Happier Here and Now

Happier Here and Now

MARY JANE GRANT

The restorative power of life's simple pleasures

CORONET

First published in Great Britain with the title
A *Cure for Heartache* in 2019 by Coronet
An Imprint of Hodder & Stoughton
An Hachette UK company

This paperback edition published in 2021

1

A CIP catalogue record for this title is available from the British Library

Paperback ISBN 9781473699663
eBook ISBN 9781473699656

Typeset in Caecilia by Hewer Text UK Ltd, Edinburgh
Printed and bound in Great Britain by Clays Ltd, Elcograf S.p.A.

Hodder & Stoughton policy is to use papers that are natural, renewable and recyclable products and made from wood grown in sustainable forests. The logging and manufacturing processes are expected to conform to the environmental regulations of the country of origin.

Hodder & Stoughton Ltd
Carmelite House
50 Victoria Embankment
London EC4Y 0DZ

www.hodder.co.uk

For my extraordinary family and wonderful friends

Contents

Message to Readers

Since early 2020, tragedies great and small have visited every person on the planet. The pandemic began as a story of loss – and continues as our shared story of learning to live anew. Moving forward, tentatively at first, we'll be asking: How do I piece my life back together again? How do I choose to live?

I faced these questions a few years ago after a painful period of personal loss. I hit a new emotional bottom that took my breath away. Slowly I found that if I could just show up in the present moment and engage with the small daily rituals of life, things began to change. I started to actively explore what worked. Day by day, moment by moment, I learned how to be happier in the here and now.

Many of us glimpsed similar insights during lockdown: It wasn't the hurly-burly of our past lives that we missed as much as the simple things – browsing in a bookshop, meeting friends for lunch, sharing hugs while gathering with family.

When 2021 dawned with faint glimmers of hope on the horizon, I thought that the lessons I learned might be of value to those asking how best to live in a post-pandemic world. The lessons are captured here, along with my personal story of love, loss and learning to live again.

My wish for you is this: As you put your life back together, I hope you will find great solace, practical guidance and a new kind of happiness in the restorative power of life's simple pleasures.

Prologue

Languedoc, France, 2015

The Peugeot took one final corner on the narrow road, and the village sign came into view. 'Labastide-Esparbairenque.'

'I'm going to learn how to pronounce that by the time I leave here,' I said to the friends who had kindly offered to chauffeur me through the French countryside to La Muse, a creative retreat set high in the hills of the Languedoc region of France. 'I've got a month to do it.'

The day before, I'd flown from Canada to Carcassonne airport, where my friends picked me up. After dinner, we sat in their living room to chat and enjoy the last few sips of local red wine. I checked my email. There was one from my lawyer: it was the certificate of my divorce. My marriage was legally over.

'It's a sign,' I said. 'I guess this is the beginning of the next chapter.'

My friends let me out in front of a rambling stone building on the edge of the narrow road, and I waved as they drove away. A tall, good-looking man with a friendly face emerged from the front door.

'Bienvenue! Welcome to La Muse.' He grabbed my suitcase and knapsack. 'I'm John, and this is Kerry.'

'Hi and welcome to La Muse,' said the pretty, dark-haired woman who came up behind him.

John and Kerry had come to France from New York fourteen years earlier to find a property that would be suitable for an artists' retreat. La Muse was the first thing they saw, and they fell in love with it. Over the years, they had turned La Muse into a comfortable place for writers, painters and musicians to work. In addition to the dozen or so bedrooms and a communal kitchen, there was a stone-walled library with a fireplace and an artists' studio with skylights. We entered through the library and went past the kitchen and up a winding stone stairway.

'Here we are,' said John. He took us inside a large bed-sitting room and put my bags down. 'Every room is named for one of the Greek muses. Yours is called Clio. The name Clio comes from the Greek word "kleos" for heroic acts. She's usually pictured with a book in one hand, so we like to give this room to writers.'

I hoped Clio would smile on me. I needed her courage to excavate my past. I thanked John and Kerry, closed the door and surveyed my room. High ceilings, tall window alcoves and a fireplace with a mantel of red-swirled marble lent an elegant air. Cracked plaster, a crooked floor and mismatched antiques offered a shabby counterpoint. I sat down at the little marble-topped desk in the window nook and looked across the gently sloping valley. The landscape was covered with the tentative pale greens of an early spring. In the sky, broad swathes of pink mingled with orange on a blue-grey canvas as the sun prepared its final descent. 'Right now,' I said to myself. '. . . Right now, I get to sit at a desk in a room called Clio in the south of France. And right now, I get to experience the magnificence of nature in a way I've never seen before or will ever see again.' Transfixed by the beauty, I felt quiet joy in that single, small, extraordinary moment.

It had been two years since my twenty-five-year marriage had come to an abrupt end. At first, I was a wreck. Bad turned to worse as the truth revealed itself. I ran away to London, to immerse myself in any reality but my own. Slowly, I started to find my way back. I tried new ways of looking at the world and experiencing life. I did research and devised experiments. In the process, I came up with six strategies that helped me, not only to recover from loss and sadness but to feel more fully alive than ever before.

I felt that the things I'd learned could help others, so I came to La Muse to write my story. It's the story of how I learned to embrace life as it happens, moment by moment, in a rich and vivid way.

For me, it has made all the difference.

1
Love and Loss

Before my marriage ended, I thought I knew a thing or two about loss. I'd been thrown into the deep end early. For the first seven years of my life, I was a happy kid living in the suburbs of Toronto with my parents, my older sister and my big brother. As the youngest, I got to spend lots of time with my mom. When she wasn't volunteering at the school or the church, she was sewing new clothes for us or painting at her easel. Her box of brushes and oils sat beside the back door, and on a sunny afternoon she'd grab them and me, and we'd head out in her Austin Mini to paint wild flowers. Many weekdays before I was in school full-time, minutes after my sister and brother had left for school my mom would say something like, 'Let's nip over to the church and see how the decorating committee is doing,' or 'Shall we see what fabric is on sale this week?' Then she'd click-click down the front hall in her red low-heeled pumps, open the drawer of the telephone table and take out a yellow pack of Peppermint Chiclets. She'd tap two Chiclets into her hand and two into mine, and out the door we'd go.

That particular autumn day started like any other. My mom sent me off to school with a kiss. Our beagle Nicky walked me to the corner. Later that morning, my mother was struck with the pain of a searing headache. She barely made it to the phone to call an ambulance, and they rushed her to hospital. It was a brain aneurysm, and she was prepped for emergency surgery. We had just enough time to race to see her before she went into the operating room. I held her hand and asked if they would shave her head. She said yes, and would I help her sew some scarves to wear while her hair was growing back? I nodded and kissed her, not knowing she had only the smallest chance of survival. It wasn't meant to be a goodbye kiss, just a good-luck-and-see-you-soon kiss, until we were together again.

She didn't make it through the surgery.

* * *

With our mother gone, our family lost the glue that had held our days together seamlessly and beautifully. I didn't know what it meant to live a day without her. The gaping hole, the terrible absence and deafening silence of life without her voice, her touch, her ever-present *thereness* was overwhelming. At seven, I knew I was sad, but I didn't know how to name that other feeling of breath-stealing heartache when the one you love simply isn't there. Not today, not the next day, nor the next, and then never. The sorrow settles over you and into you and then it becomes part of you – a vacancy you carry with you for ever.

'Wait!' I'd protest silently. 'I want my mom to see me win this race . . . I need her to help me sew my first dress . . . I want to race home to tell her I came first in my class.' But life didn't wait, and I had to do all those things and so much more without her.

On the day of my mom's funeral, the church overflowed with people. I was the only one wearing white in a sea of black. My mom had made the dress for my first communion. Some of the girls had stiff, scratchy crinolines that made their skirts stick out like flying saucers. Mom knew I hated itchy fabric. My dress was made of soft cotton. Hundreds of tiny gathers at the waist helped the skirt ease out ever so gently. If you looked closely you could see that the dress was covered in tiny embroidered eyelets. I loved that dress. After my mom died, I loved it even more, because when I wore it, I felt like she was with me.

My mother was buried in Holy Angels Cemetery on the far edges of Toronto. There was a flat bronze marker on the grave. I worried that we would never find her in those acres of buried people. I asked my dad why my mother didn't have a proper, tall gravestone, but he didn't answer. I thought she should have a monument with her hobbies engraved on it – a sewing machine, a paintbrush, maybe her Austin Mini. Then we could find her again.

My father was lost without our mother. I think that's why he made the rash decision to remarry. He just wanted a normal family again. But it didn't work out that way. He left the family business he'd been part of for his whole life. We moved out of our cozy home and into a creepy old house. We were briefly happy when our little half-sisters came along, only a year apart. But our life was descending into chaos and our father's health started to deteriorate. Less than five years after our mother died, we found ourselves back at the funeral home, this time to say good-bye to our father.

I scanned the crowd for my sister and brother, but I couldn't find them. My stepmother was sitting at the back of the room. People occupied a little knot of chairs around her. She had black circles under her eyes, either from too little sleep or too much mascara mixed with tears, or both.

In the weeks following my father's death, our phone was buzzing with calls. The family had to work out what to do with us. Then, we were told: the two little ones would stay with our stepmother, while my sister, brother and I would be split up among different aunts and uncles.

Why didn't I feel relieved? The years of chaos and confusion were over.

But now I was losing the rest of my family. I went to my baby sisters' room. The older one was awake. She held out her arms, and I picked her up. We sat together in the rocking chair, and I covered us both with a blanket. 'Sing Beatles,' she said, snuggling against my chest.

'Michelle . . .' I sang, and the tears streamed down my face. I cried for my mom, who would have given anything to be there to comfort me. I cried for my dad, who got swept away by life. I cried for our family, because we were about to fall apart for good.

And I cried for myself, because I didn't want to say goodbye to everyone I loved. And because I had to learn, too soon, that nothing is for ever. Those you love and need most can send you to school with a kiss on a sunny autumn morning and be gone for ever by the afternoon. We don't get to say when love goes. It just goes.

Decades later, on a warm October day, Stuart and I said *I do* with all the confidence of newly-weds. *We'll be together for life. Our love is strong.*

And ours was, for twenty-five years. We worked, took trips, moved from the city to a small town, had a wonderful son, a cat and a dog, lots of friends. We almost never fought and if we did, we'd quickly and carefully resolve our differences. There were small challenges but nothing we couldn't work out. Our marriage was happy. Was it too happy? Maybe it was boring.

One bitterly cold Sunday morning, Stuart and I were sitting in front of the fireplace in our beautiful home. Our town, set on the shores of Lake Ontario, had recently been named the prettiest in Canada. I was doing the weekend crossword puzzle. Classical music was playing. The dog was at Stuart's feet; the cat was curled up beside me. Too good to be true, you might say. Turns out it was. Because that's when Stuart leaned forward and said he wanted out. Didn't want to be married any more. I couldn't understand. Please explain, I said. What's wrong? Since when? His words sounded vague, rehearsed, unreal. There didn't seem to be a convincing explanation.

We separated, and I told myself this was a test of our marriage, that we'd find our way back together again. I was glad our son Ryan was out on his own, living in London now. I found a small one-bedroom apartment in Toronto, imagining it would become our city pied-à-terre once Stuart and I reunited, as I was sure we would. But that was my secret. Meanwhile, Stuart helped me move. He installed dimmer switches, put in under-cabinet lights, hung the paintings. We made multiple trips to IKEA, and he assembled the shelving units. He was acting the role of dutiful husband, making sure I had everything I needed.

Then, it was done. I walked him to his car. We hugged and said goodbye. I remembered kissing my mom and hugging my dad, not knowing it was for the last time. Which was worse – knowing or not knowing? Stuart cried. I couldn't tell if they were tears of sadness or relief.

I came back to the apartment, closed the door, sank to the floor and wept.

Later, I poured a big glass of wine and went out to the balcony. I could see over the treetops and across the lake. Tiny sailboats leaned into the blue water.

Fresh tears came, and the breeze felt cool against my wet cheeks.

One month went by, and then another. It was early autumn when the story revealed itself. There was someone else. He wanted to be with her, not me. It was that simple.

I felt stupid for trying so hard to convince myself that we'd reunite. I felt the shame of being rejected after so many years together. And for the first time in decades, I felt the unmistakable, gnawing pain of knowing that someone I loved was gone for good.

Suddenly I was desperate to get away. I needed to immerse myself in distractions. I decided to go to London, England. I could see my son, and we could spend Christmas together. I could live somewhere else, and maybe even pretend to be someone else.

Anyone but me.

Anywhere but here.

2

The Pleasure of the Senses

Languedoc, France, 2015

My leg moved across soft linen and stretched into the cool, empty side of the bed. Where was I? I opened my eyes to see the cracked plaster of an ancient wall: I'm at La Muse, in France. It's the beginning of a creative adventure.

I kicked back the covers and let the chilly air hit my skin. My feet swung down into fuzzy warm slippers. I was armed against the quirks of this beautifully decrepit building with its cold floors and draughty windows.

Throwing a sweater over my pyjamas, I opened the heavy drapes. The light and sounds of early morning seeped in. Little voices chirped, and I peered down to the old stone patio. Kerry was there with her three kids, hanging wet sheets on clothes lines that stretched from tree to tree to tree. The weight of each sheet brought the lines precariously close to the muddy ground underneath.

'Here, Mummy!' The twin boys each took one end of a sheet and stretched it wide so Kerry could hang it up. They

held it as high as they could, and she helped them lift it over the line. Then, she guided the sheet as it settled down, one side even with the other.

'Thanks, boys!' Kerry said. 'Now, get your backpacks. We're leaving for school as soon as I hang the rest of the clothes.'

Kerry reached into the basket, pulled out a pink T-shirt and draped it over the line. Seven-year-old Sophie held up a clothes peg. Kerry took the peg and rested her other hand on the little girl's shoulder.

'Thanks, sweetheart. You're a wonderful helper.'

Kerry and Sophie finished hanging the laundry, took one handle each of the empty basket and headed inside.

I went down to the kitchen, and made coffee the French way, in a small pot on top of the stove. As I poured the coffee into a wide ceramic cup, steam filled the air with a rich aroma. I added a splash of milk, and an irregular cube of brown sugar, and stirred it with a bent silver spoon. I popped two fat slices of yesterday's baguette into the toaster. Minutes later, I slathered them with sweet butter and tart marmalade. I alternated bites of toast with nibbles of soft, yeasty goat cheese. Was there a more perfect meal?

After breakfast, I went to my room and sat down at the desk in the window to finish my coffee. Inhaling deeply, sipping slowly, savouring the taste, I welcomed my awakening senses. My eyes rested on the soft pale green of the trees, about to burst into full leaf on the hillside across the valley. My mind went back to November 2013 and the day I left Toronto for a two-month stay in London . . .

Toronto and London, November 2013

While sitting in the departure lounge at Toronto's Pearson International Airport, I noticed the middle-aged couple across the aisle. She was reading *People* magazine and sharing tidbits of celebrity gossip. He responded with the odd raised eyebrow or murmur of 'You don't say,' while continuing to scan his newspaper. The tips of their boarding passes protruded from the front pocket of her purse. It was a chunky thing made of faux leather, black with white top-stitching. There were several zipped compartments where I assumed she stowed all their important documents, both his and hers. The strap was long enough to go over her far shoulder. I imagined her making a special trip to buy that purse, so she could foil the thieves she expected to encounter around the tourist attractions in London. The purse was practical, but not pretty.

Down from me and across from them sat a girl, maybe twenty-five, wearing short boots and a mini-skirt. Her legs were bare. 'She must be cold,' I thought. Her purse was an open sac, everything mixed up and exposed. She didn't notice when the middle-aged man glanced over his newspaper at her. Does he fantasise about her? I wondered. Then the wife followed his line of vision. Is she miffed that he let her catch him looking at a girl the same age as their own daughters? He snapped his newspaper and lifted it higher. His wife fixated on the girl's open jumble of a bag. I could hear her thinking, 'I hope the London pickpockets don't nab that wallet or the phone, tossed so casually in there.'

Stuart and I used to travel like that couple. I made the plans, booked the tickets, printed the boarding passes and carried the documents in my functional purse. But that was no longer my role. I'd become one of the 'brave' single ladies, travelling solo. I didn't want to be that practical middle-aged woman any more, but I wasn't about to be a silly girl. Where did I fit?

In London, I found the bed-sitting room I had reserved through Airbnb. It was located inside a huge apartment owned by a friendly woman who lived there with her two teenaged daughters. I didn't share their family space, but I liked the fact that my room was securely tucked inside their home. I didn't feel quite so alone.

The flat was in a nondescript 1970s brick building about four storeys high. But the location was fantastic, just inside the exclusive enclave of Primrose Hill while bordering on the edgier Camden Town.

My room was just large enough for a double bed, dresser and desk with a small chair. One vertical half of the single closet was for clothes; the other half was taken up by shelves over a small fridge. That, and a kettle, would be my kitchen for the next couple of months. Off the room was a clean, modern bathroom with lots of counter space and a heated towel rack. Luxury! A big, frosted window over the bathtub lifted wide open to a short view across a narrow lawn.

Once I was settled, I met Ryan for dinner at the local pub. Over a beer for him, glass of wine for me, and a platter of fish and chips, we talked. He told me he was okay that his father and I had separated. But how are you, really? I asked. He assured me he was fine. Not surprised. Even a bit relieved for us. My intelligent and insightful twenty-three-year-old son said that maybe we weren't all that well suited anyway. That I might find somebody with whom I shared more interests, especially on the intellectual side. Maybe a professor.

We laughed. I made sure he knew we could talk about his dad or the separation or anything he wanted, any time. He said he would.

Dinner over, he walked me to my building, gave me a hug, said goodnight and headed down the street toward the Underground. I watched as he dug into his pocket and pulled out his phone. Arms cocked, I could tell he was catching up with texts and calls. I'm not sure why, but that made me feel he was okay.

Concerning my larger circle of family and friends, I had asked them not to mention or write to me about Stuart while I was in London. Removing him from my day-to-day existence was part of my rewiring project – I needed to lay down new tracks in my brain and my heart, so they weren't on constant alert for the sound of his name or news of his life.

The next few days I made tentative forays into London. I walked through beautiful Regent's Park to the affluent neighbourhood of Marylebone, where I poked my head into shops and popped into cafes. I joined the throngs on Oxford Street, mesmerised by the gorgeous displays in London's famous department stores. More streets, museums, cafes . . .

One problem: I was there, but I wasn't.

The vibrant city of London was at my feet, and I was barely taking it in. Seeing something remarkable, I would instinctively reach out my hand to touch

Stuart's arm and say, 'Will you look at that?' But my hand sliced through thin air. Nobody there, no complicity in the beauty of the moment.

I felt the sting of rejection. 'You've been discarded, remember? He doesn't want to share his life with you. She's there now.' And so, moment after stunning moment – bells ringing in St Mary's churchyard, birds chirping in counterpoint, sunlight sneaking through the trees to play against the stone wall – barely registered before I retreated inside my head. Experiences that were vivid when shared seemed to evaporate when perceived alone. Gone! Was it real? Was I there? Did it matter?

I wandered the streets of London, while my mind replayed past conversations in a relentless search for the clues I must have missed. Other times, it tortured me with images of my husband and his new girlfriend together in our home. How did she feel waking up on my side of the bed? Did she see the beautiful old oak reaching up into the morning sky? Could she spot the cardinal in the crab-apple tree in our front yard while she stood at the bathroom sink? Maybe right now, she was sitting in my little black chair in front of a warm fire, knee to knee with Stuart, talking about the day or making plans. Perhaps she was leaning forward for a kiss or to hear him say, 'I love you.'

My mind held me prisoner. When it wasn't dragging me through endless loops of the past, it was taunting me with heartbreaking scenarios about an uncertain future.

One afternoon, lost in thought, I stepped carelessly into Camden High Street. A sickening sound of screeching tyres filled the air.

'Do you wanna get killed?' a driver yelled from the window of his black cab. He'd come to a stop just inches from me. I looked at him, and tears sprang from my eyes.

Maybe he felt sorry for me. He pointed at the kerb and wagged his finger.

'You Americans!' he said. 'Be careful over here! Remember – you look right!' He drove away, and I sank back into the crowd on the sidewalk. I put one foot in front of the other with care. Why was I doing this to myself? Wasn't I in charge of my thoughts?

Shouldn't I be able to turn them off? I desperately wanted to get out of my head.

I headed toward the safety of my little room. I turned onto the Parkway – a commercial stretch connecting gritty Camden with the outside edge of upscale Primrose Hill. The Parkway had a little of each: posh shops like Whole Foods sat alongside basement jazz clubs, hip coffee shops and cheap pizza chains. I walked slowly, with my head down. The dampness of the sidewalk penetrated the soles of my black boots. I thought about the cliché that dampness gets into your bones and chills you. I shivered.

Then, a rush of warm air hit me as two ladies emerged from a tea shop. They turned in the direction of Primrose Hill, laughing and chatting in comfortable camaraderie. I envied them, having a friend to meet for afternoon tea, before going home to make dinner for their husbands. The seductive strains of self-pity started to play in my mind.

'Stop!' I shouted silently to the voice in my head. I grabbed the handle of the door to the tea shop, pulled it toward me and stepped inside.

I came face to face with a display of little white pots arrayed on the counter. Each one was half filled with loose tea – some mostly brown strands, others in more colourful blends of buds, leaves and dried flowers.

'SMELL THE TEAS.' A laminated sign was propped beside the pots. On closer inspection, I could read more: 'Blends. Beautiful tea blends. SMELL THE TEAS. Pick up the little cups.'

I felt like Alice in Wonderland. I obeyed the sign. I picked up one little cup labelled 'Tranquillity'.

'Just what I need,' I thought to myself as I lifted the cup and smelled. The unmistakable scent of lavender hit me first. But, what else? Something citrus, possibly. Something musty . . . I closed my eyes. For now, it was just the smells. I let them fill me up as I breathed slowly, in and out. After a minute or two or three, I opened my eyes to survey the contents. Tiny buds of pale purple revealed the lavender, while small yellow bits of dried lemon peel answered my question about citrus. These were set among nondescript leaves and stems. Another sign sat on the counter with the tea names and their descriptions. Under 'Tranquillity' it listed lavender, lemon, lemongrass, Egyptian chamomile and Pai Mu Tan white tea. I thought these ingredients would fulfil the promise of tranquillity perfectly.

I picked up the next tea because I liked its pink hues. I could see red peppercorns, chilli flakes, burnt ochre threads of something and other pieces in shades of cream and brown. I closed my eyes and raised the little pot to inhale. 'Warm,' was my first reaction. 'Spicy' came next. 'Sweet,' was a possibility. One thing I knew for sure: the smell of this tea took me somewhere exotic and exciting. Only then did I open my eyes to look at the name of the tea. 'Chilli Chilli Bang Bang.' Ha! I loved that name. I laughed out loud. What was in it? Cinnamon, ginger pieces, red thistle, chilli flakes, sweet red peppercorns and rooibos tea.

'One more,' I thought. But how to choose? One of the teas was displayed in a white bowl, centre stage. It must have been the feature of the day. 'Old-Fashioned', it said. 'I don't want to be old-fashioned,' I thought.

But I liked the look of it. Bright reds, warm oranges and soft greens stood out against a black backdrop of tea leaves. Let's see . . . I recognised peppercorns and was quite certain about the bits of orange peel, and the green looked like either lavender or rosemary. I lifted the bowl and let the aroma waft my way. 'Okay, it's rosemary definitely,' I thought. 'And the tea, it's strong.' I closed my eyes and was transported to the beach, back home in Canada, on the shores of Lake Huron. We were sitting around a campfire. My toes were buried in the sand for warmth, and my eyes were transfixed on the flames. Wow.

I opened my eyes and came back to the tea shop in London.

'May I help you?' A young man approached me from behind the counter. He was smiling.

'I think I'd like a cup of this, please,' I said. 'I'm not sure why it's called Old-Fashioned, but it smells amazing.'

'It's one of our most popular teas,' he said. 'It's super smooth, classic and sophisticated.'

I liked the idea of being classic and sophisticated.

'Perfect,' I said. 'By the way, where does the campfire smell come from? Or is that just me?'

'You're right,' he said. 'It's the lapsang souchong tea we use as the base for this tea. The leaves are dried over pinewood fires. There's nothing else like it.'

While he made my tea, I scanned the list of ingredients: orange peel, rosemary, pink peppercorns, red cornflowers with lapsang souchong and keemun black tea.

I ventured further into the tea shop. Along the service counter were platters of baked goods. Scones, brownies, cookies, cakes and more. An apple-spice muffin seemed like the right choice. I ordered that along with the tea and, a few minutes later, the young man brought my tray to the cash register. There was a small white pot of tea, nestled on top of a matching cup and saucer. On the side of the plate holding the apple-spice muffin, he had added a generous dollop of pale English butter.

'Why not?' I said as I paid and picked up my tray.

'Exactly,' he said, looking pleased that he had added a splurge I would not have taken myself.

I made my way into the seating area, a jumble of mismatched tables and chairs. 'Boy, this place puts the 'shabby' in shabby chic,' I thought. I found a small round table with a wooden top and a white base, its paint peeling from the wear and tear of many pairs of feet resting on it day after day. A formal dining chair had been painted high gloss white and upholstered in fresh, floral chintz. The walls were covered in different wallpapers – a bamboo motif ran up against a botanical theme sitting next to a bold geometric pattern. In some areas, the brick wall was exposed. The light-hearted chaos of the place appealed to me.

While the tea steeped, I split open the muffin and spread butter across the warm, crumbly surface. I watched the butter melt. I took a bite. Memories of my grandmother's kitchen came back. Smooth, soft pieces of apple added tiny bursts of flavour. The creaminess of the butter brought everything together into a rich and spicy experience.

Now for the tea. As I poured, the scent filled my nostrils while leaving my forehead damp with steam. I closed my eyes and imagined I'd been invited into the country home of an elegant and generous friend, to sink into a down-filled, chintz-covered couch in front of a roaring fire on a damp autumn day. And then to taste . . . Citrus and spice mingled with smoky bass notes.

I alternated bites of the apple-spice muffin with sips of tea. I cradled the smooth white cup in my hand, ran my fingers over the uneven top of the time-worn wooden table. I looked around the place and watched the people.

Time passed. Eventually, my plate held only crumbs, and my teacup had but a few damp leaves at the bottom. I tipped the pot – it was empty. I looked at my watch and realised that an hour had passed since I first saw the sign telling me to smell the teas. And, all this time I had been possessed of neither sad memories nor anxious worries. I was completely and simply here, with the tea, the place, the people, myself.

I was present.

And it felt wonderful.

After a while, I put on my coat, picked up my tray and carried it back to the counter. The young man was busy assembling pots of tea for customers. He looked up and gave me a friendly smile.

'See you soon.'

'You bet!' I replied.

I stepped outside and continued toward my room. It was getting dark. Instead of looking down at the sidewalk, I looked up at the faces of people coming in the opposite direction. Sometimes my eyes met theirs, and I must have been smiling because several of them smiled at me. I wanted to stay in the magical mindset I had found in the tea shop. The place of right here and now.

'Cool air,' I said to myself as the damp evening chill touched my cheeks.

'Spicy curry,' I said, catching an exotic aroma as patrons entered an Indian restaurant.

'Raindrops reflecting.' I described light bouncing off black cabs, still wet from an afternoon shower.

'Listen.' The sounds of a London rush hour swirled around me. Car engines running and revving, punctuated by the occasional beep of a horn. Workmates saying goodbye as they turned in their respective directions home; friends saying hello as they met up outside the pub. People on their mobile phones, walking and talking, some animated, others in low tones, a melange of languages. Kids in school uniforms zipping by on skateboards and scooters.

For the duration of my walk home, I clung to the five senses. Labelling helped. What I felt, heard, saw, smelled – I kept saying words, often out loud. 'Cool. Damp. Warm. Green. Spicy. Bright . . .'

I had no idea why it helped, but it did. What I knew for sure: my foray into the senses freed me from my mind. For the first time in months, the hamster wheel was still. Obsessive thoughts, disturbing worries, soul-parching scenarios of what a lifetime of loneliness might look like . . . These were refreshingly absent.

Instead, I had taken an expedition to the exotic land of tea, savouring its smells and relishing its flavours. I felt my grandmother's embrace and a friend's warmth as I tasted the comforts of apple and spice. My eyes enjoyed a visual collage of bricks and chintz and wood and people. I listened to the sounds of London and really heard them, possibly for the first time. Whatever this new world was, I wanted to explore it further. Through an accidental event, I had been able to experience the simple pleasure of what was happening at that moment without the chattering commentary of an anguished mind.

How had something as basic and accessible as the five senses had such an impact? I was hungry to learn more.

I woke early the next morning, and the lessons of the previous day drifted into my awareness. Eyes closed, I lay on my back and swept my legs across the sheets, like a snow angel on smooth cotton. My toes probed the unoccupied corners of the bed. Lazily I continued, back and forth. 'Warm, cool, warm, cool . . .' I whispered to no one.

I liked the sound of my voice, still a little hoarse from its eight-hour idleness. 'Sexy,' I said, then giggled. Is a voice still sexy if there's no one there to hear it? I rolled onto my side and hugged the pillow. Slowly, I opened my eyes. 'Wedgwood blue,' I said as my fingertips traced the shapes of pale-blue figures against the creamy background of the soft sheets. It reminded me of my grandmother's china. During those many summers long ago, when we visited my grandparents in Nova Scotia, we always had dinner in the wood-panelled dining room, where my grandmother brought out her beautiful Wedgwood china every day. She didn't save it for special occasions. To her, every day was special. I let my eyes rest on this familiar pattern while my hand brushed against the fleecy fabric for a few more minutes.

Then, a slow, distant rumble. I sat up on the edge of the bed and reached forward to pull back the curtains. The rumble grew louder.

Suddenly, swathes of colour streaked by. Rushing behind the high hedge at the back of the property was a commuter train. Then, as fast as it had come, it was gone, pulling the sound behind it for a few seconds more. In the sudden stillness, foreground colours stood out. The mixed greens of the hedge, from pale to intense, settled before my eyes into a tranquil still life.

Continuing my morning routine, I let my senses wake me up.

'Cool mint,' as I brushed my teeth.

'Cold tile,' when I forgot my slippers before entering the bathroom.

'Smooth and sweet,' as I took a big spoonful of creamy oatmeal into which I had tossed a handful of fresh blueberries.

As I felt the pop of blueberry between my teeth, a sudden image came to me – Stuart and me at the farmers' market. We always waited for the wild blueberries to come into season, and when they did, we added them to everything. Cereal, pancakes, muffins, even salads. Thoughts arose: 'What's he doing now? Is she there? Did he mean those things he said to me?' But something was different this time. I found myself looking at my thoughts in a curious yet disinterested way, as I might watch clouds in the sky. I saw them, then let them float by. I felt the burden of worry recede with them, and things seemed brighter and clearer. And so, I walked back into my life, free to experience what came next, and then what came after that.

After breakfast, I decided to go to the library. There were things I needed to know, and I figured the local library would be a good place to start. On the way there, I noticed the streetscape. Interspersed between elegant white houses were facades painted in peony pink, butter yellow, sky blue and hues in between. The remains of faded flowers tumbled from window boxes. It was tranquil and beautiful. I reached the library and entered.

'Good morning!'

The cheerful middle-aged woman standing behind the counter in the large foyer was attractive in a way that some people call handsome. Her strong face was framed by black-rimmed glasses. Her thick, straight white hair was cut in a perfect line that grazed her shoulders. She was the type featured by fashion magazines, to encourage woman my age to let their hair go grey. I was trying, but my natural colour was emerging in shades of putty and cement. A sludge of dull neutrals. Nothing like this elegant shade of platinum. She wore a large silk scarf, swirling with pinks and reds, in perfect contrast to her dove-grey cashmere sweater. She didn't look like a typical librarian. I guessed she was a volunteer, a long-time denizen of Primrose Hill.

A handmade sign on the left of the counter said 'Returns' and one on the right said 'Check-Outs'.

'Good morning,' I said. 'I'm just here to do some reading. Is that all right?'

'Of course. And you are visiting from . . .?'

'Canada. Toronto, actually. I'm here to write and spend time with my son. He lives in Islington. I'm staying just down Gloucester Avenue.'

'Lovely. And welcome.' She smiled as she gathered up the books from the 'Returns' side of the counter. I caught the subtle scent of perfume as she walked by to put the books back on their proper shelves.

I entered the reading room. Morning light streamed through tall windows. The walls were filled from floor to ceiling with books, and a dozen or more free-standing shelves took up much of the remaining space. To the left of the entrance door were counters with computer stations. Above, a bulletin board was covered in notices, local advertisements and sign-up sheets for classes and lectures. A couple of round wooden tables filled the rest of the space. People sat here and there, reading books and newspapers. I went to an empty table, quietly unpacked my things, sat down and closed my eyes.

I could hear the occasional rustling of a newspaper and the soft hum of the heating system.

I took a deep breath through my nose. I detected a faint floral hint from the hand lotion I'd applied before leaving my room. Lately, I'd switched my allegiance from lavender to rose. Maybe it was the influence of England. After all, what was more English than a rose?

I settled into place, opened my laptop, connected to the Internet and started my search.

My first question was simple: why, when I immersed myself in the present, did I feel so much better? By pulling my attention to the five senses, I had given myself no choice but to focus on what was happening in the moment. I was not stuck in the past or worried about the future. Yesterday, I had learned first-hand that the senses held the key that opened the gate to my present experience. They admitted me to the garden of earthly delights – sights, sounds, smells, tastes and physical feelings – right here, right now. By being in the body, I could calm the mind and soothe the spirit. It felt neither self-indulgent nor hedonistic. It felt beautifully, blissfully ordinary.

So, what was so special about being in the moment? Perusing the Internet and the library's bookshelves, I came across inspirational passages and quotes. Walt Whitman said it poetically: 'Happiness, not in another place but this place . . . not for another, but this hour.' The philosopher Henry David Thoreau said, 'Live in the present, launch yourself on every wave, find your eternity in each moment.'

'Yes', I thought. 'Good. I understand. But was there current research behind these proclamations?'

Then, I found some: a rigorous 2010 study published in *Science* magazine used smartphone technology to gather over 250,000 data points while tracking the ongoing thoughts, feelings and actions of 2,250 people every moment of the day. The findings were startling: respondents spent almost half their waking hours thinking about something other than what they were doing, and this typically made them unhappy. In the words of the authors, 'A human mind is a wandering mind, and a wandering mind is an unhappy mind.'

'If this is true', I thought, 'then the reverse must also be true: we are happiest when we are paying attention to what we are currently doing.'

There was scientific support for why I felt more at ease and more content when I managed to stay in the moment. And other studies concurred. But what about the power of the senses to bring us to this place? And why are we so poorly tuned to the nature of our sensory experience, when it sits quite literally at our fingertips?

Some people suggest that our increasingly manufactured and indeed virtual world is causing us to lose touch with our senses. It seemed to me that we tend to either ignore our senses or overload them. Sometimes we stuff our senses, pound them with loud music, gorge them on too much food, overpower them with artificial fragrances and assault them with violent movies – to the point of numbness. Our poor senses – whether numbed or calloused – are taken for granted.

In her classic, *A Natural History of the Senses*, author Diane Ackerman described what I was beginning to realise – the senses are our tangible connection to life. 'There is no way in which to understand the world without first detecting it through the radar-net of our senses.'

The senses bring us into the moment; they also connect us to our minds and our hearts. Not in distracted cogitation or emotional diversion, but in the manner of alert discernment and acute feeling. The modern philosopher Richard Kearney tells us that Aristotle pronounced our sense of touch as the most universal of the senses. In his work *De Anima (On the Soul)*, Aristotle says touch is intelligent because it is literally sensitive. When Aristotle says, 'Touch knows differences,' he is speaking to our fundamental capacity to discriminate and therefore think. Tactility is both sensorial and cognitive.

The tea shop. My hand lotion. A burst of blueberry on my tongue. I knew from my experience of the last twenty-four hours that the senses transported me through a lifetime of feelings and memories and into the present moment. And I was beginning to understand that the senses also had the power to divert the mind from the monotony of endless rumination – in essence, to reset and reshape our thoughts. My senses were delivering me bodily, intellectually and emotionally into the present. They refreshed my capacity to be a fully integrated human being in the here and now.

As personal and immediate as my senses felt to me, I started to appreciate how they were also universal and timeless. We are connected to others through the common bond of the senses.

I thought about the poets and painters who struggled to connect us with this shared experience called life – through brushstrokes designed to replicate the wonder we feel when confronted with an exuberant bouquet of sunflowers, or through words carefully chosen to remind us we can see the world in a grain of sand and heaven in a wild flower. Artists implore us to look, to listen, to smell, to touch and to taste this life, while it is within our capacity to do so.

I loved the idea that the senses are both personal and universal, immediate and timeless. They connect us with our own life, and with every other life. As Kearney suggests, when music stirs our soul or when we feel kindness we are likely to say, 'I have been touched.'

I looked up from my reading. Everything had changed around me. The people who had been there when I first sat down were gone. New ones had arrived. A murmur reached my ears from the far side of the room, where three ladies sat together, sharing the day's news in easy conversation. The light coming through the tall windows was brighter now, and the angle of the shadows had shifted. I looked at my watch. How did it get to be early afternoon?

I closed my eyes and sat still. I felt enormous gratitude to my senses. Every moment of every day, whether I was aware or not, they worked to connect me to the beauty of the world and the universal experience of humankind. Our senses are the unsung heroes of a life well lived. Paying attention to the senses is not indulgent; it is intelligent. It is, in fact, the only way to live – fully connected to the world and one another.

Right here. Right now.

I returned to Ackerman's work and paused on this: 'So much of our life passes in a comfortable blur. Living in the senses requires an easily triggered sense of marvel, a little extra energy, and most people are lazy about life. Life is something that happens to them while they wait for death.'

The choice was stark and real: I could continue to stumble through life, my mind elsewhere, my senses dulled, my heart aching for what wasn't here. Or, I could live right now. To stop long enough to see what lay before my eyes, to take in the simple sounds, smells and tastes of an ordinary day, to touch and feel the tapestry called life. And in so doing, to bring all of myself – body, mind, heart and spirit – alive.

Slowly, I gathered my things. My hands were shaking. Was it hunger, excitement, possibly awe? I laughed to myself and thought, 'I'll bring the excitement and awe along to lunch while I deal with the hunger.' I headed toward the exit.

'Did you find what you were looking for?' I turned to see the attractive woman who had greeted me earlier.

'Yes, thanks. And much more.' I smiled, pushed open the door and stepped into the fresh air of an English afternoon.

Happier here and now: bring the pleasure of the senses into your everyday life

Label your experience as it happens. *'Cool,' when a fresh breeze hits your bare arm. 'Comfort,' when you catch the scent of bread baking. 'Sweet,' to welcome the warbling voice of a child singing. Labelling your senses brings you into your body, and when you are in your body you are in the here and now. Negative emotions about the past (regret, sadness) and the future (worry) tend to fade when you anchor yourself firmly in the present moment via your senses.*

Do a five-senses deep dive. *Take an apple from the fridge: Feel the cold, smooth skin against your palm. Look at it closely. How many colours and textures do you observe? Lift it to your nose. What is it about the smell that makes it apple-y? Close your eyes and listen to your first bite. Notice how the scent intensifies. How does the apple taste? A regular five-senses deep dive will deepen your appreciation of all the simple, everyday pleasures that we take for granted.*

Take your senses for a walk. *When you walk, act like a tour guide for your senses, doing things that awaken each one in turn. Run your fingers along a rough stone wall, taste the rain on your tongue, smell the freshly mown grass... Revel in what you see, hear, smell, taste, and feel. Connecting to the multisensory vibrancy of your surroundings can make you feel intensely alive right here and now.*

3

The Pleasure of Wandering

Languedoc, France, 2015

I loved early mornings at La Muse. Waking at dawn, I lingered in bed to relish the feeling of soft linen sheets against my skin and heavy blankets on my body. I listened to the birds and peeked out from under the covers to watch the morning light penetrate the shadow.

One morning, I threw back the covers, put on the same clothes I'd worn the previous day and headed out for a walk.

The village was quiet. Somewhere in the valley, in one of the little makeshift enclosures dotted along the river, a rooster crowed. I let my fingers trail along the sides of damp stone walls and twisted twig fences.

I followed the narrow main road of the village as it swooped toward the river before bending back up to an old stone wall at the base of a tall hill. Cold spring water poured continuously from a small pipe, and I cupped my hands for a quick drink. I stayed with the road as it worked its way back through the heart of the village. Steep pathways veered left and right, up and down, to houses that were tucked long ago into every inch of available space.

I returned to La Muse, lungs refreshed by the morning air, thirst quenched by the spring, and my mind's eye still enjoying the colour and texture of the village and the valley below. The kitchen was empty. I quickly put together a coffee pot and placed it on the gas stove. When the pot hissed loudly, I switched off the heat and poured steaming coffee into a large mug. A bit of sugar and milk, and I was ready to head up to my room. The warm mug felt good in my hands, still chilly from the walk.

I sat at my desk and looked out the window. 'Pale green,' I said, scanning the trees which were ready to burst into leaf. 'Fresh,' I said as the smell of laundry wafted up from the clothes line. 'Busy,' I said as the air filled with staccato chirping from the wee birds assembled in the ivy. 'Cool,' as my forearm brushed across the marble top of the desk. I took my first sip of coffee. 'Ah . . .'

Happier Here and Now

London, November 2013

During those early days in London, I did everything to live through the five senses. 'Blue,' I'd say as I woke up to the Wedgwood-patterned sheets. 'On time,' to the sound of the morning commuter trains rushing along the tracks behind my building.

It worked. Whenever I got tangled in the past or started worrying about the future, I'd come back to where I was and what was around me. 'Misty,' to the London morning. 'Wet,' when the raindrops caught me by surprise.

Now that I had awakened my senses, I wanted to get out and delight in the elements. I started to walk everywhere. The senses were helping me feel more present and alive. What would happen if I took that feeling on the road, literally? Could I maintain it or even enhance it? By bringing a new level of awareness to the practice of walking, could I learn things I had not anticipated?

One Sunday morning, I decided to walk from my little flat in Primrose Hill to Hampstead in the northern reaches of London. It was just over two miles, mostly uphill. I had travelled only a few blocks when I met a cheery French fellow in a blue striped apron, standing in front of his fish shop. He had set up a small table, on which sat a wide-mouthed stainless steel bowl brimming with ice, seaweed and fresh oysters. Beside that was a tin bucket with more ice and several cold bottles of Chardonnay Sur Lie. The fishmonger was offering samples to everyone who came along. When I arrived, an English chap wearing tweeds and hiking boots was balancing a small spaniel in one arm while eating an oyster from its half-shell with the other hand. He dropped the empty shell into a bin under the table and reached for a glass of wine.

'How wonderful,' I thought. 'It's barely eleven thirty on Sunday morning and we're scarfing oysters and wine on a sidewalk.'

The fishmonger handed me a large Irish rock oyster, and a poured a generous sample of wine. The plump oyster glistened. I lifted the hard shell with its uneven edge to my lips and slurped. I felt a slippery sensation against my tongue before I bit once, then twice. My taste buds sprang to life.

'Salt . . . Sweet . . . The ocean!'

I remembered the words of French poet Léon-Paul Fargue, who said eating an oyster was 'like kissing the sea on the lips'. Each chew released briny sweetness. Then, the wine. I closed my eyes and lifted the glass to my nose. A fruity bouquet transported me to vineyards and orchards. I took a sip and let the wine sit still in my mouth. The flavour of apples and pears mingled with the lingering sweetness of the oyster. I swallowed.

'Vanilla . . . Butter . . . Intense.'

My senses were dancing. The cool, silky feel of the oyster was followed by the taste of land and sea. Ocean smells wafted from the fish shop while church bells rang in the background.

We three – a tall Frenchman, a dapper Englishman and a small Canadian woman – stood on the sidewalk and chatted. After a while, I said goodbye and carried on along Gloucester Avenue. I was glad I had taken the time to stop. In the past, I might have smiled and walked on, focused on reaching my goal. Today was different. I had a destination, but it was in soft focus. How or when I reached Hampstead was of no concern to me. I wanted to take my time. Diversions were welcome.

By stopping and tasting and connecting with two humans and a dog, I experienced an unexpected pleasure. Time seemed to slow down. Some philosophers and even scientists believe that haste and speed can accelerate time and cause it to pass more quickly. Might the converse also be true? Perhaps time expands and slows when it's allowed to do so. Frédéric Gros, author of *A Philosophy of Walking*, says, 'Days of slow walking are very long: they make you live longer, because you have allowed every hour, every minute, every second to breathe, to deepen, instead of filling them up by straining the joints.'

I zigged and zagged my way through Primrose Hill, enjoying the whimsicality of the pastel-coloured townhouses. I headed in the general direction of Hampstead but did not plan the route. Now more than ever, I wanted the journey and the day, the space and the time, to simply unfold. Anything could happen. I felt an immense calm. The passing landscape – parks, churches, people, shops, children, dogs, birds and buses – arose in front of me and then fell behind me. I could appreciate what Rebecca Solnit said in her book *Wanderlust*, 'Part of what makes roads, trails and paths so unique as built structures is that they cannot be perceived as a whole all at once . . . They unfold in time as one travels along them.'

'Is that a metaphor for our journey through life?' I wondered. No matter how much we plan and worry, we can never see around the next bend or beyond the moment at hand. So why do we spend so much time poking into the dark, unseen and never-to-be-known corners of a future we can never control?

So far, the notion of taking my senses for a walk was working. They were heightened – perhaps by the volume and variety of stimuli, or because I had set out with my sensory antennae high. Immersed in the green of the trees, the cool of the air, the scent of autumn leaves and the hum of traffic, I had nothing to do but walk and feel the simple pleasure of moving through the world in this moment.

I turned onto Eton College Road and admired the stately buildings as I made my way to Haverstock Hill. This route would take me to Hampstead. My leg muscles felt the uphill grade as I passed through Belsize Park, Rosslyn Hill ... As I moved north, the environs became less urban with a little more breathing space. I could imagine when these neighbourhoods were villages on the road from London to the countryside.

As I reached Hampstead High Street, the tantalising aroma of sausage frying in butter came from a little alley off to the side. I joined a long queue of people to a small trailer with a sign that said La Crêperie de Hampstead. Twenty minutes later, I gave my order to another tall, friendly Frenchman. His colleague was an equally statuesque French woman. They worked together with ease. Two hot circular griddles, side by side. She ladled batter on the first one, and while it cooked, she finished the crêpes on a hot grill behind her. When her crêpe neared golden brown, she flipped a large knob of butter onto the round griddle in front of him and flipped her crêpe over to his side, where he spread the ingredients

– cheese and ham for me, lemon and icing sugar for the two little girls ahead of me. Once everything melted, he folded the crêpe expertly into its cardboard cone, wrapping that in layers of napkins. I took my crêpe, found an empty spot on a bench and sat down to eat, nibbling away the light, crispy exterior until I reached the gooey filling on the inside.

When I stood up from the bench, I had no sense of time. I was simply there, in a singular time and place, and it felt perfect. Ambling down the road toward home, I turned onto side streets. My senses brought me to each moment: the smell of fire from brick chimneys, the sound of kids playing, the visual orderliness of trees marching in a straight line along the street. As much as my body was present, as evidenced through my sensory reality, so was my mind, but there was a new texture of mind. The never-ending script that had been my constant companion, so full of babble and interior dialogue and worry and what-ifs . . . all this had been nudged out of the frame by a quiet awareness, a simple noting of this and that and a most welcome peacefulness that was new to me.

I experienced a deep sense of balance, which gave me an appreciation for Rebecca Solnit's words: 'Walking, ideally, is a state in which the mind, the body and the world are aligned, as though they were three characters finally in conversation together, three notes suddenly making a chord . . . It leaves us free to think without being wholly lost in our thoughts.'

I was thinking, but in a much more fluid and present way. It was as though thinking were another one of the senses – and just as sounds, sights and smells arose and fell away, so did my thoughts. They came, and they left. They were not even 'my' thoughts so much as they were simply 'thoughts'. Just as I could identify and note a smell as 'that's fire' or 'there's bread baking', so I could note a thought as 'that's a sad memory' and 'there's an interesting idea'. It was a new lightness of thinking, where I was not lost in or attached to my thoughts. I connected this experience with what I had been learning about mindfulness and the benefits of acceptance and non-attachment. In their book *Mindful Learning*, Craig Hassed and Richard Chambers say, 'Whatever is happening is happening.

There's no denying that. At one moment there is comfort, peace, success or happiness. Enjoy it, but remember that it will change so don't get too attached to it. Equally, if there is an experience of pain, anxiety, failure or even depression, then so be it. Be patient – that too will change. Life constantly teaches us that experiences – both pleasurable and painful – come and go whether we like it or not.'

What they called 'experiences' – peace, comfort, pain – could just as easily be labelled thoughts and feelings. I liked experiencing them vividly and then letting go. Be here fully for what is happening, and then let go, to be here for what happens next. If you cling to a moment because it is pleasant, you will miss the new moment. Why did the experience of walking bring this insight to life for me? It seems the physical act of moving through space and time brought it together in a way I could not have discovered using my mind alone. I was stringing together the moments in unison with my step. Step, step, step. Moment, moment, moment. The experience of here followed by here, now followed by now.

A few days later, I returned to north London on an expedition to Highgate Cemetery.

The morning was foggy and cool. Arriving at the gates, I expected to encounter a formal place, with orderly rows of grand monuments marking the lives of an impressive roster of illustrious residents. Instead, I entered a space like nothing I had experienced or expected. Pathways snaked through a disordered profusion of wild greenery and decaying gravestones. There was a tragic beauty to the overgrown graves, evidence of the inevitable forgetting and eventual neglect of those who languished unaware beneath.

The eerie beauty of the place beckoned me to venture deeper. I surrendered to the path, and whenever it broke into multiple branches, I let my feet choose the way. As I walked, I sank further and further into the environment. The damp air penetrated my skin, and I was enfolded into the place. I could feel almost no distinction between me and the mist, the trees, the moss and the broken stone. In this place of death and decay, I was filled with the immediate experience of being alive. And yet I felt less distinctly me. I was not only present in the here and now, but I felt as though I was present in all of space and all of time at once. Was it the companionship of the dead that invited me to mingle with them across the limitation of time? Was it the seductive mystery of the place that drew me into this immediate experience of being an indistinguishable part of the whole? Whatever the catalyst, this feeling of being alive and yet less distinctly me filled me with quiet joy and effortless ease.

'Who is this "I" anyway?' I wondered. It seemed that the more I tried hanging on to the 'me-ness' of me, the more likely I was to suffer or worry. The lighter my grasp on myself, the lighter I became in my mind and my heart.

Going back to my senses, I noted that perceiving something in this way was accomplished naturally, without anyone making the experience happen. The smell of coffee could drift across the kitchen and reach my nostrils. My olfactory sense would take it in, and a sensation needing no label (but which I will label now as 'the smell of coffee') would register. Perception happens, and awareness happens. There is no director, no narrator, no 'I' directing the fact that something is happening. It simply is.

Once we comprehend that this illusion of self is a mental pattern that rises and falls, we can watch this sense of the self come and go in the same way we allow events, things, thoughts, feelings to come and go. We can loosen our grip on the specialness of the self and sense the freedom in doing so.

At Highgate Cemetery, I stepped off the path and went closer to the gravestones. I loved the simplicity of the headstone of Douglas Adams (1952–2001), who wrote *The Hitchhiker's Guide to the Galaxy* and then died too young. The headstone of artist Patrick Caulfield (1936–2005) was carved in the same pop art style for which he became famous in his lifetime. 'Did he carve it himself?' I wondered. 'Was this his final work, his own tombstone?'

How long does a legacy last? How many people remember Adams or Caulfield today? How far down in the footnotes of time will they be fifty years from now?

And what about Elizabeth Jones (1846–1901)? During her short life, she didn't create a body of illustrious work or engage in brave acts that put her in the history books. Chances were slim that a single person alive today would have a clue about her.

The famous and the unknown, side by side, equally dead, for ever. The names, mostly forgotten. The span of dates – all too short. Life is short. It's crazy, over-before-you-know-it short.

Most people would agree that we are not alive before we are born, and we are not alive after we die. Most of us would also agree that we were alive yesterday and we expect to be alive tomorrow. Of course, it's obvious. But what isn't so obvious is this: you can't *be* alive yesterday you can't *be* alive tomorrow. Yet, we spend so much of our time there. A great portion of our mental and emotional resources is channelled into a past that's gone and a future that never comes.

Sometime in the afternoon, I left the cemetery, cut across Hampstead Heath and started the long descent down Haverstock Hill back to my flat. I grappled with this thought: it isn't that an average life is eighty years long. You don't live for eighty years. You live today, and then today and then today. You don't live yesterday, you don't live tomorrow, and you can't live eighty years all at once. You can only be alive for one moment at a time. The moments might add up to eighty years, but you can only live them one at a time. Therefore, life is only one moment long. This moment, then this one, then this one. So, it's wrong-headed to say 'Life is short. Make the most of the years you have.' We should instead say, 'Life is short. Make the most of this moment. It's all you've got.'

You can only do this thing called living right here, right now. It will only, always and for ever be today.

This seemed suddenly obvious to me, but why had I lived my life up until now as though something else were true? As if it were worth my time to think about the past? As if tomorrow mattered more than today? I realised I spent most of my time designing a future life while forgetting to live the current life – the only life – I have. I wondered why I invested so much into a distant future that I believed would be better than today. So many of my todays had played second fiddle to an imagined, glorious tomorrow.

If there's a tragedy to living in the past, there's a futility to living in the future. But that's where many of us live.

The brilliant philosopher Alan Watts saw this in the mid-twentieth century when he wrote his 1951 classic *The Wisdom of Insecurity: A Message for an Age of Anxiety*. In it, he said, 'To pursue (the future) is to pursue a constantly retreating phantom, and the faster you chase it, the faster it runs ahead . . . To understand this is to realise that life is entirely momentary, that there is neither permanence nor security, and that there is no "I" which can be protected.'

Rather than be alarmed by this thought, my experience in the cemetery taught me to be comforted by it. I remembered the experience of stretching across time and space to become part of a greater whole, a unity of everything and everyone that ever was and ever will be. There was more freedom and security in that feeling than I could ever achieve by trying to hold on to anyone or anything, ever. Nothing endures and yet it all endures because it's part of something bigger. The pieces and indeed the people come together and then fall apart, grow and then decay, are born and then die. But the whole remains whole. And we are part of it, for all time.

The simple act of walking helped me experience moment-by-moment awareness. Step, step, moment, moment. The five senses helped me engage in the vivid reality of now. My immersion in the world of Highgate Cemetery created a lasting feeling of connectedness with everything. The gravestones reminded me that life is short, and that life only comprises this moment. There is only one place – here – and there is only one time – now – in which to live. If you can manage to stand fully present in the intersection of here and now, you are hit with a vitality and freshness that stuns you.

The graveyard also reminded me to maintain an acceptance of death. Knowing that 'I' do not really exist in the first place, and that this thing I call 'myself' is an illusion, and that as far as I do exist, I am an indistinguishable part of a whole – I am not as fearful of death. If I am part of the whole, there is no beginning or end to me anyway.

Perhaps this is a paradox, but even if I am one part of a whole, I still want to make my part, my experience of this thing called life, as good as I can. If my life is only one moment long, how do I choose to live each moment? It is this decision and only this decision that will shape my life. If I am always ready with a kind word, then I will live a life of kindness. If I am quick to offer a warm embrace to someone who is lonely, then I will live a life of compassion. If I ask 'why' then I will live a life of curiosity. If I stop to savour beauty, then my life will be lifted by what is beautiful. I can't be kind tomorrow or hug someone yesterday, but I can do it now.

Happier here and now: bring the pleasure of wandering into your everyday life

Walk every day. *When I had a dog and walked for an hour a day no matter what, I learned one thing for sure: You will never regret going for a walk. In fact, it feels especially fantastic to come home after braving bad weather, because (a) you did it and (b) it makes home all the more welcoming. Make a daily walk part of your life. You will feel physically energized, mentally refreshed, and emotionally more balanced.*

Walk somewhere new. *Visit a different part of town or an unexplored green space. You don't have to go far to find a patch of newness. It's about giving yourself the gift of seeing something for first time, which will bring you into the present moment, where we feel most alive. A fresh perspective might spark creativity and help you reframe old problems in new ways.*

Get a little bit lost. *Allow yourself to explore unfamiliar territory without an agenda or a map. It will turn your excursion into an adventure, and you'll be amazed by what you find. Serendipity – when something happens by chance in a beneficial way – might even deliver a pleasant surprise! A small step outside your comfort zone might leave you feeling excited by new possibilities.*

4

The Pleasure of Letting Go

Languedoc, France, 2015

Reluctant to leave the comfort of my warm bed at La Muse, I started to keep yesterday's clothes at hand, so I could quickly dress and head outside without thinking. It didn't take many days before I was rising at dawn and walking in the early morning light.

'Warm,' I said one morning, thankful when the sun hit my back. 'Awake now,' I said when the rooster's piercing cry startled me. 'Beautiful,' I said when my eyes came to rest on a small, stone building not far from La Muse. A rough wooden door was painted dark red, and the latch was fastened with a thick, worn stick that curved in such a way as to hold the door securely closed. It was exactly right for the job. Signs of ingenuity were abundant throughout this tiny village. Homes, barns, huts, fences – all were built with materials provided by nature, all of it close at hand. I could see where repairs and adjustments had been made, using branches, vines, maybe a bit of plaster, and more stone. The

villagers were merely shaping nature, bending it ever so gently, to meet their needs. Houses softened into the landscape because they were made of the landscape. Handmade fences and sheds were imperfectly perfect. How could they be anything but?

As I approached the spring where water flowed freely, an old woman was walking down the hill from the village. Her steps were slow but sure. She wore sturdy brown leather shoes laced over thick cotton socks. Hand-me-downs from a dead husband? Her bowed legs disappeared under a shapeless plaid skirt. I counted three layers of mismatched sweaters. She was up before anyone else in the village and walked every morning to the spring for her daily water supply. I slowed my steps, not wanting to interfere with her routine. She made her way across the stone path in front of the spring and, with her feet planted wide apart, she squatted down to slowly fill her Evian bottle. When did she buy that one bottle of Evian? And how many times has she refilled it? I thought about life at home in North America, where it was normal for one person to consume and discard a half-dozen bottles of water in a single day.

In our shared kitchen at La Muse, life was simple. We threw our leftovers together to make the soup du jour, *a melange of flavours. That soup, with a little bread and cheese, would serve everyone for lunch the next day. I liked how we had fallen into this habit of sharing leftovers, so everyone got fed and nothing went to waste. It was far more fun to figure out how to make things last than to buy more, and how to use every bit of something rather than throw it out.*

London, November 2013

I came to love my tiny home in Primrose Hill – the bedroom with its small desk just big enough for my laptop, a kitchen consisting of a bar fridge and kettle, and the bathroom with its long tub and wide window. I hadn't brought much with me either – two pairs of jeans, one casual skirt and a few sweaters.

I'd been in London only a few days when my friend Leslie called.

'What are you doing tonight?' she asked.

'No plans,' I said.

'Good. Then you're coming to the fundraiser. The princess will be there and a few other members of the royal family. My friend just cancelled. She told me to give her ticket to someone, so I'm inviting you.'

'But, I don't have anything to wear,' I said. Besides, I wouldn't know anyone, and I wasn't feeling very sociable.

'It's ten o'clock in the morning, you're in the middle of London and you have a credit card,' said Leslie. 'I'm sure you can come up with something!'

She was right. The party was an opportunity to get out and have fun. My excuses were lame.

'Okay, thanks,' I said. 'I'll be there!'

I called Ryan.

'Do you want to take your mom shopping? Leslie's invited me to a black-tie event tonight.'

'Sure!' Ryan said. 'Let's start in my neighbourhood. Upper Street has all kinds of great shops.'

Ryan and I agreed to meet in an hour. I took the Underground to Angel, where he was waiting. We started along Upper Street, looking in one shop after another. An hour passed, we'd found nothing and I was getting a little worried. I owed it to Leslie to show up.

'I have a good feeling about this place,' said Ryan outside the next shop.

Inside, I thumbed through the racks and stopped at a little black dress made of light wool, cut in a slim silhouette. The neckline was finished with a band of dark green fabric flecked with silver.

'Perfect!' I said. 'Now, let's hope it fits.'

I tried it on and it looked like it had been custom made. Ryan gave it two thumbs up.

I bought the black dress, and we carried on along Upper Street. In the window of a thrift shop, I spotted a pair of black suede high heels. They fitted perfectly and cost almost nothing.

'Okay, Cinderella's ready for the ball!' I said. I hugged Ryan and headed home to prepare for the evening.

After showering and doing my hair and make-up, I put on the dress. It looked perfect, paired with my string of pearls, sheer black stockings and the suede high heels. I felt good, for the first time in months. I even felt pretty.

I was feeling a little nervous when I arrived at the party. I found Leslie, who introduced me to a few people before she moved off to greet other guests. Realising my hostess was busy, I started to chat and mingle. As the evening went on, I even felt a little of my old confidence coming back. I had a wonderful time.

'By the way, I love your dress,' said Leslie when I found her to say goodnight and thank you.

What happened next came as a surprise. I started to wear that little black dress everywhere. I wore it to join friends for a drink, to meet Ryan for lunch, then on a solo excursion to the Victoria and Albert Museum. Another day I put it on with flat black boots and went to work in the British Library. I could make the dress look fancy enough for a black-tie event, or simple enough for a day in the stacks. In my previous life, after its initial debut this 'special occasion' dress would have hung unworn in the closet for months, maybe years. But now, with limited choices, I pressed the dress into service time and again. And every time I wore it, no matter when or where, it reminded me I was living a full life in this fantastic city and doing it all with so little. Jeans for comfort, sweaters for warmth and a little black dress for every other occasion. I started to wear my grandmother's pearls too, every day, no matter what. I liked the idea that my todays met her yesterdays in this unbroken strand of shared moments. I had everything I needed, no more and no less. Even my bedsit served me well. Using the kettle, I made oatmeal in the morning and tossed in some fresh fruit. The small fridge held cheeses, olives and fruit and vegetables for lunch and dinner. I wrote for hours at the little desk and sat on the comfy bed, my head propped up on pillows, to read.

It had been six months since I'd moved from our large family home to a one-bedroom apartment in Toronto. In making that move, I had to choose what to take and what to leave behind. I had already started the process of living with less, and I found I liked it. This experience in London, in a way, took the experiment to the extreme, and it helped me see not how limited life could be, but how free I could feel with few possessions.

My calendar was about as empty as my closet. Unlike the years I'd spent as a wife, mother, caregiver, consultant, teacher, carpool member, committee chair, volunteer, dinner party hostess and so much more . . . now I could choose how, where and with whom I would spend my time. Ryan was a priority. As were the handful of friends I had in London. And my work. But what was rising in importance was the idea of keeping plenty of white space in the calendar.

I was starting to feel something like freedom, and it was the reverse of the 'go-go' state I'd lived in for most of my adult life. I had become so accustomed to racing from one obligation to the next, and adding possessions to the pile, that it was only now, in looking back, that I could see how buried I had been in stuff and busyness. Sarah Susanka, author of *The Not So Big Life*, says, 'There are two major culprits responsible for our feeling overwhelmed. One is the accumulation of things we think we need; the other is the speed at which we race through our days.'

Stuff and speed. Accumulation and achievement. We've got so much stuff that we buy books to tell us how to get rid of it. What's wrong with this picture? And our poor days, filled to bursting with our endless to-do lists. There was no doubt that this condition had come to define so many lives, but how did we let it happen?

We say we are seeking to be happy. The irony is that not only is the carrot always out of reach, but the process inevitably backfires. We're so busy grasping at what we think we want and chasing so-called happiness that we barely have a chance to experience what is happening.

My recent experience of mindful walking had taught me that the only way to be present was to let go of both the past and the future, but now I was seeing that the opportunities for letting go were much greater. What if we could let go of all the wanting – not just wanting things and experiences but wanting life to go a certain way, to go 'our way'?

By planning and working and striving, we feel we are controlling events. But it's an exercise in self-deception. We are surprised again and again when our best-laid plans are shoved aside by an unexpected and sometimes unwelcome reality.

Another explanation for piling up stuff and obligations is found in our search for meaning. The more things we accumulate and the more we accomplish, the more meaning we believe our life must have.

And so, we grasp and hold on for dear life. John Parkin, author of *F**k It*, says, 'Anything that has meaning for us – anything that matters – carries the potential to cause us pain. Meaning is a brightly coloured box with pain inside. And sometimes – without us wanting it to – the lid just bursts open and the pain comes pouring out. The problem is that meaning – things mattering – is attachment. And anything that we're attached to has the potential to turn round and bite us.'

So, stuff doesn't make us happy. We don't control anything. And meaning equals attachment equals pain.

A change in circumstances pushed me from my family home to an apartment, and then to an even smaller space in London, carrying few possessions and making only rare commitments. I was feeling freer and happier than I had felt when I energetically chased happiness and meaning. Living lightly, I was starting to sense what it felt like to simply have, do and be enough.

But could I take this small life with me?

I began with the question of stuff. When I moved back to my real life in Toronto, how might I resist the temptation to add possessions? Could I consider the possibility of shedding even further?

I was inspired when I read about the baseball player Daniel Norris. Recruited to the Toronto Blue Jays for a $2 million signing bonus, he chose to live out of a van during training camp in Florida as a conscious effort to keep his life simple and not let his new-found wealth corrupt his values. He said, 'In my mind there's no need for luxury, or at least society's sense of the word. I consider my life luxurious – I live on a beach with an oceanfront view, hearty meals and hot French-pressed coffee at my disposal. That's fancy, right?'

I thought about my preconceived notion, that to have a beachfront view and other lifestyle luxuries required a supersized income and large expenditures. Yet, here was a guy who had the money, and chose to live this way. It really is a choice, and we have more access to life's real 'luxuries' than we may think at first. What's better than a good meal, a strong cup of coffee and to rest in nature? I'd been learning this through slowing down and savouring the gifts of the senses. Now I was starting to see that it didn't take much more than that to live a rich and full life. Simplicity delivered all the benefits with less of the pressure.

I turned to one of my favourite books and a much-loved classic, *Gift from the Sea* by Anne Morrow Lindbergh. She stepped out of her busy life as a wife, mother and journalist to spend a few weeks in a simple cottage on the beach. There she discovered how it felt, really felt, to pare back to the essentials: 'One cannot collect all the beautiful shells on the beach. One can only collect a few, and they are more beautiful if they are few . . . For it is only framed in space that beauty blooms . . . A tree has significance if one sees it against the empty face of sky. A note in music gains significance from the silences on either side.'

I loved the idea that we need to leave space – and time – around objects and events if we want to experience them truly.

So, what about time? How could I maintain the white space in my calendar? How might I let go of the illusion of control over time and its outcomes? I thought about what I'd learned during my walks through Highgate Cemetery. I'd come to realise that we can only experience life at this moment. Not in the past and not in the future. Life is always and only happening now and so how we live our life is determined by what we choose to do in this moment. If we choose to be present, there is the possibility we might experience time as that singular, unfolding moment of rich and vivid experience. When we rush from one obligation or activity to another, or when we live in the past or the future, it is more likely that time will feel out of reach or like a relentlessly ticking clock, its sand running through the hourglass until time is 'all gone'.

It struck me that I had spent most of my life with a completely inaccurate understanding of time. Until now, I had believed time was a limited resource that had to be managed if one were to live a successful life, by 'getting everything done', for example. I'd spend an enormous amount of effort trying to 'save time'. In so doing, of course, I was putting pressure on myself. I'd thought if I could just do this one thing faster – or better still, do three things at once – then I'd be somehow 'ahead' of time. By ploughing through the to-do list faster, and therefore 'saving time', I'd assumed I was somehow banking a block of future time to spend exactly as I wished. Maybe I'd even occupy that special time in a state of presence and awareness. Two things happened: the to-do list was never done, which meant the special block of time was never reached. And I was so busy striving toward the future and playing my imaginary control games with time that I was rarely, if ever, present in the moment.

As dire as this realisation felt, I was excited about what it might mean to get past my old conception of time. I thought, 'If I can't really save time, that must mean I can't spend time or run out of time. I will never have less time than I have right now, and I will never have more time.' I sat with this idea, and then I laughed. 'That means I have all the time in the world!'

Coming at it from a slightly different angle, Sarah Susanka said: 'When you are really at one with the unfolding of every moment, the experiencing of time is very different from the way we usually think of it. Real time seems neither long nor short, neither instantaneous nor eternal. Now is experienced not as time but as presence, and though we are aware of flow, it's as though its duration is incidental; it barely touches us.'

At first, I thought she was saying that time is an illusion. But then I looked at it more obliquely and saw something else: by saying 'now' is experienced as presence, it seemed she was saying that 'now' really means 'here'. I had always thought of 'here' as space, and 'now' as time. If they were overlapping, it struck me that this moment must sit at the intersection of space and time. Could I bring my presence, attention and awareness to the here and now, while allowing the moment to unfold?

I liked the idea of getting out of the way if only to see what might happen.

One unseasonably warm day, I was strolling through the beautiful streets of Primrose Hill. The sun illuminated the whimsy of the pastel-coloured houses, pinks and blues and greens jostling playfully along the pavement. I turned the corner onto Chalcot Road, and the tantalising aroma of garlic and butter wafted in my direction. The irresistible smell was coming from a tiny corner bistro called L'Absinthe. I'd been there once with Ryan, and on this sunny midday I thought, 'Why not?' I had no plans – no obligations – and the little bistro was calling my name.

'*Bonjour*,' I said to the owner Jean-Christophe, known as 'J-C' to the locals.

'*Bonjour*,' he said with a smile. 'Welcome back! Table for one?'

J-C sat me at a small wooden table tucked into a quiet nook. I wasn't all that comfortable eating alone in restaurants, so this extra bit of privacy suited me. I considered the menu: one could choose from two soups (French onion or leek and potato), two salads (lyonnaise or green salad), two main courses (steak frites or coq au vin) and two classic desserts – crème brûlée or lemon tart. I loved the simplicity of the menu – just a few choices from a small array of equally appealing options.

J-C came by and popped a small glass of wine in front of me.

He winked. 'With our compliments.'

I smiled and thanked him. I ordered the salade lyonnaise. A few seconds later, a small French baguette appeared on the table. I tasted the wine and broke off a piece of baguette. 'Warm,' I said. My fingers felt a bit greasy. I took a bite. The inside of the baguette was flaky and moist with the taste of salted butter. I leaned against the back of the wooden chair and looked around the bistro. I was completely present, and it felt absolutely right. J-C moved about with ease, stopping to chat and joke with his regular customers, making each person feel welcome. He wasn't in a hurry. He did whatever came next, in a manner of pure effortlessness and enjoyment.

My eyes moved around the room. The decor was simple – warm yellow walls with a sweet border of hand-painted names of classic French dishes: 'Crème Caramel', 'Jambon Cru-Rémoulade', 'Cassoulet', and so on. I looked to my right and spotted the phrase meant to be 'Boeuf Béarnaise.' Whoever had painted it forgot to include the first letter 'a'. Instead of repainting it, they had simply painted a small letter 'a' above the word and indicated with a flick of an arrow that this was meant to be in the word. I loved this sweet mistake, left unselfconsciously in place for all to see. 'I'm not perfect,' it said. 'And why would I want to be?'

I thought about all the striving I was leaving behind. For much of my life, I had been trying to have it all, do it all, get 'better' every day, aim for perfection, create a more beautiful home or fashionable wardrobe or plumped-up résumé. Slowly but surely, I was moving away from that, toward a state that simply felt like 'enough'. Sitting in a little bistro on a warm autumn day, sipping wine and nibbling on baguette – I felt gratitude for this gift.

And there was something else. Being in that place and time – at the intersection of here and now – without an agenda or the need for things to be a certain way, I belonged to the moment. Mindfulness expert and author Richard Gilpin says that when we attend to the ordinary moments of daily life, 'a quiet and miraculous adjustment takes place and ... the ordinary becomes extraordinary.'

J-C brought my salad, and we exchanged a smile. The greens glistened under a warm dressing, and the scent of fresh tarragon rushed up to greet me. Yes, it was enough – and richer than anything I had ever experienced.

Happier here and now: bring the pleasure of letting go into your everyday life

To let go of things, ask two questions: Is it useful? Is it beautiful? *Take your inspiration from nineteenth century designer William Morris and aim to own only things you love because they are either useful or beautiful. This will set you free from keeping things for the wrong reasons.*

How many ways can you use the same thing? *My black dress taught me that a single item can go a long way. Try it yourself: wear a special occasion item in an everyday setting. Notice how you feel. (Also notice that no one else cares!) Or wear one outfit for a week. Apply the test to more possessions. You might find yourself clearing out things that don't earn their keep!*

Protect the white space in your calendar. *Letting go of things is simple because it's concrete. Letting go of striving, busyness, saying yes when you mean no – is harder because it's more abstract. Whenever you are tempted to add an event or obligation, ask yourself if it reflects what you want your life to be about.*

Deepen your understanding of time. *There is no such thing as a perfect tomorrow when you can start living the life you intend. Tomorrow never comes. All you have is right here, right now. So, whatever you mean to do in your life – today's the day to start!*

5

The Pleasure of Doing What You Love

Languedoc, France, 2015

I reflected on why I had come to La Muse. It had been two years since the end of my marriage, and a little over a year since I had gone to London – first to escape, then to find my way back. In London, it took a while to establish my emotional footing, helped along in large part by my experiments in living more mindfully. Now, at La Muse, I wanted to capture the essence of what I'd learned. In coming here, I hoped to make the swathe of creative time wider and more open. By definition, a retreat is a place where days are uncluttered, and time is expansive. If you're lucky, the mind follows and becomes clear-thinking and wide-ranging. I sought this quality of mind to help me look back on what happened and what I'd discovered in London.

From my desk, I looked across the valley at trees tinged with the green of spring and abandoned terraces from centuries-old gardens. I watched birds land on the ivy that climbed across the red tiled roof in the foreground of my view. The sun threw tracks of light on distant hills; it would reach back to warm our side of the valley as the hours passed. Here, time flowed naturally without interruption, and I found myself going deeper, lingering on questions, allowing ideas to emerge. A strong focus was balanced by a sense of ease.

At La Muse, I was settling into a new rhythm of work, something I first experienced in London . . .

London, November 2013

I'd been in London almost a month and was starting to feel alive again. I thought back to the early days when I was lost in anxious thoughts and painful feelings. After some trial and error, I had made my way back, first through the senses, then through long, meandering walks across London, and more recently by reflecting on what it meant to let go of things, of obligations and more. As I experienced new sensations through my experiments, I wanted to learn about what was happening. I started to read more and deepen my research. I loved alternating between action and reflection, doing and learning. It took my work beyond rational, analytical thinking to a place where sensations, feelings and intuition came into play. Electrified by the flow of new insights and hungry to learn more, I set out to explore the nature of work itself. What happens when you immerse yourself in work you love? How might work enrich our lives? Ideas and questions were percolating and popping and bubbling.

One morning, I left the pristine streets of Primrose Hill and walked down gritty Camden High Street toward the British Library. I came upon it – a massive yet beautiful red-brick building, set far back from busy Euston Road with an expansive piazza out front. Opened in the 1990s, this new British Library was not only the largest public building constructed in the United Kingdom in the twentieth century; it was the largest library in the world, with over 200 million items in its collection.

'No better place to learn,' I thought as I crossed the square, looking up to see a hulking bronze sculpture of a primitive man hunched over geometric tools. 'Inquiring minds,' it suggested to me. I inhaled the aroma of fresh coffee from the courtyard cafe, opened the heavy front door and entered the library.

The first order of business was to apply for a Reader Pass, which enables qualified researchers to use the library's reference materials and work in its Reading Rooms. I was directed to the administrative area on the lower level, where I filled in the requisite forms and handed them to a friendly red-haired chap behind the desk. He asked me a few questions about my research and told me to come back in an hour.

While I waited, I wandered through the building. I was transfixed by the book-filled glass tower standing six storeys tall in the centre of the building. A security guard told me the column contained 65,000 printed volumes dating from 1763 to 1820, all from the personal collection of King George III. I felt the wisdom in those books, brimming with the ideas of thinkers through the centuries. I perused the items on display in the main floor gallery, impressed by the collection of precious materials ranging from the Magna Carta to Leonardo da Vinci's notebooks to hand-scribbled song lyrics by Lennon and McCartney. I could hardly comprehend that original works of such diversity and significance were gathered in a single place. I had a cup of tea in the cafeteria and immersed myself in the quiet hubbub that surrounded me. When the hour was up, I returned to the lower level.

'Here you go,' said the young man I had seen earlier. He handed me my Reader Pass. 'Now, you can get to work!' He seemed as excited as I felt. I smiled and thanked him as I took my pass. Following his instructions, I went to the cloakroom in the basement. Most of my belongings went into a locker, and I put my wallet, laptop, notebook and a pencil into one of the library's clear plastic bags. Coats, umbrellas and pens weren't allowed in the Reading Rooms.

I found the Humanities Reading Room on the second floor. At the door, a security guard reviewed the contents of the plastic bag and approved. I surveyed the room and its long rows of oak carrels with green leather work surfaces and upholstered oak chairs. Natural light came through an atrium, and the floor was covered in wall-to-wall carpet. The room was nearly full. Hundreds of people worked in concert, each one focused on a unique line of enquiry. A studious quiet filled the air, punctuated with an occasional cough or whisper. I saw an empty spot, settled in and started to write in my notebook. I found myself feeling incredibly grateful for the luxury of space and time to do the work I loved – writing, thinking, researching, learning.

I could see that the void created by the loss of my marriage was now available to be filled with something new. And that something was the opportunity to do work I loved.

I realised that sometimes the prelude to doing good work, even inspired work, can be loss. A significant loss not only creates space, it alters perception, changes feelings, shifts thoughts, makes anything possible. It also says that even great things we had never dared dream might be possible too. I thought about the poet John Keats, who lost his family early, as I had. His father died when Keats was eight, his mother when Keats was fourteen, and his beloved brother Tom died of tuberculosis when Keats was in his early twenties. After his brother's death, Keats went on to have his 'annus mirabilis', writing many of his most beautiful works, including 'Ode to a Nightingale'. He also developed a uniquely powerful poetic style that would eventually place him among the great lyric poets of the Romantic era. Artist, innovator, creator – finding inspiration in a void of loss.

In a more modern context, the gifted food writer and editor of *Gourmet* magazine was stunned when the magazine to which she had dedicated her career was abruptly shuttered. In shock, Ruth Reichl turned to what she knew and loved best next to writing – cooking. She says, 'My kitchen year started in a time of trouble, but it taught me a great deal. When I went back to cooking I rediscovered simple pleasures, and as I began to appreciate the world around me, I learned that the secret to life is finding joy in ordinary things.' During what began as a period of mourning, she not only cooked and learned to look at life in a new way, she wrote a thoughtful and beautiful memoir about the experience.

During those days in London, I could feel myself entering the void to stretch and explore. I began to do the work I loved best – reading and researching and writing. I wanted to know what others had to say about what I was experiencing – everything from the power of the senses to the workings of the mind, and so much more. I wrote pages and pages to examine my thoughts, explore new insights and play with ideas. I did not realise it at the time, but I was writing myself into the next chapter of my life.

A new routine took shape. I rose early and walked from my flat to the British Library, where I took my spot in the Humanities Reading Room. My days acquired a sense of purpose and focus. I was gaining traction and engaging with life again.

Reading the diaries of the twentieth-century writer Anaïs Nin, I appreciated how work can literally and physically connect us to life. Describing her experience of operating a manual printing press, she said:

'The words which first appeared in my head, out of the air, take body. Each letter has a weight. I can weigh each word again, to see if it is the right one.'

It is in the process of doing work – whether it's the mental work of pulling words from the air or the physical work of arranging metal letters to bring those words into existence – that we can connect with life's creative force and the art of manifestation. Whether our work is mental, physical, social or something else, it's energy made real.

While my work at the time, and through much of my life, has been primarily through the intellectual faculties, I love to think how physical work connects you to the senses. When the mind and the body come together with real focus, there can be an incredible connection with the present moment. Immersed in work, we engage with life's creative force, often unaware of much else. Philosopher Alain de Botton observed this as he watched an artist at work. He describes it this way: 'At these times, he is nothing but a mind and a hand moving across a square of canvas. Past and future disappear as he is consumed by the tasks of mixing paint, checking its colour against the world and settling it into its assigned place in a grid . . . There is no more ten in the morning, no more July, but only the tree before him, the clouds above, the sun slowly traversing the sky and the small gap between one branch and another, whose resolution and completion will constitute a whole day's work.'

Through his work, this artist is deeply connected – to the beauty and specificity of nature, to his thoughts and ideas, to his hands and fingers, to his tools and materials – as he strives to bring all these elements together and say something about his experience of life in that moment. If he succeeds, he might create one of the great works, which capture the essence of what the artist experienced in that moment of focus and connection.

As I spent my days reading and thinking and writing, I felt a deep connection with something – creativity, a stream of consciousness, life . . . I can't say for sure, but I know it brought a feeling of satisfaction and meaning that had been missing in recent months.

This sense of connection started to expand. As I sat in my study carrel, I was aware of the people on either side of me and across from me, and in the rows of identical desks that lined the light-filled space. Each of us was focused on our work, formulating hypotheses, generating ideas, tracking down what others had said or written about our topic of interest. We were working individually, and yet we were part of a shared energy.

'This is where I belong', I thought. 'These are my colleagues. We share the quest to know something more than we did yesterday, to propose a new way or idea, to conjure up a pattern or theory.'

As I read I wondered about where and how these thinkers had worked through the ages. In my undertaking, I had joined a community – the one here and now at the library, but also the one that reached back through time and space.

American writer and humanitarian Wendell Berry described the sense of community that work can give us: 'Good work . . . graces with health . . . By it, we lose loneliness: we clasp the hands of those who go before us, and the hands of those who come after us; we enter the little circle of each other's arms, and the larger circle of lovers whose hands are joined in a dance, and the larger circle of all creatures, passing in and out of life . . .'

The thought that work had brought me into a community of like-minded seekers – past, present and possibly future – gave me a wonderful sense of connection. I hoped that my little fragment might find a home and perhaps a meaningful role to play in the larger context. Maybe I could contribute a new perspective, something that's been missing? Who knew?

Dancer and choreographer Martha Graham said: 'There is a vitality, a life force, an energy, a quickening that is translated through you into action, and because there is only one of you in all of time, this expression is unique. And if you block it, it will never exist through any other medium and it will be lost.'

I loved this quote because it lent humility to the notion that our work might be special. The specialness comes, by definition, through its uniqueness, nothing more. Whether it be through research and writing or through painting or community work or entrepreneurship or daily care for a family and loved ones, whatever we choose to do, and however we choose to do it, is the one and only way that particular bit of universal energy is going to be expressed – now or ever. If we don't do it, it will be lost. While this could make one feel guilty or pressured, it made me feel alive with purpose and focus.

Working in the library with hundreds of others helped soften the feelings of isolation that had defined my recent past. And knowing that my fragment of work might form part of a larger effort, stretching back through the centuries and reaching forward in time, also gave me a sense of connection. The idea that my efforts might unlock a unique voice and a contribution lent both urgency and humility to the task. Finding one's purpose through work, and losing one's self in the process of doing it, was a beautiful paradox that I was experiencing for the first time.

While I loved the new rhythm of my working days, I was still living very much alone. A couple of times a week, I met with my son or with one of the few friends I had in London, but the bulk of my time was spent in solitude. I reflected on what I had learned about letting go of obligations and commitments. Letting go created freedom, but freedom to do what? Now I could see that it had created the freedom to work and live in a new way.

My pace of life was different. I left lots of white space in the calendar and time for rest, reflection and refreshment. On my days at the library, I took time at lunch to enjoy a real meal – not a rushed snack at the desk as I'd done most of my life. The library itself helped me learn this lesson: food was forbidden in the Reading Rooms, and there was a fantastic cafeteria on the top floor. They must have known that thinking creates an appetite because the meals were hearty and delicious. Every day I'd head up there to peruse the options: piping hot meat pies with gravy and roast vegetables, crispy fish and fat potato wedges, velvety soups, glistening salads, dark chocolate cakes, English puddings with rich sauces . . . I loved it all and ate with relish. Taking my time, I focused on the experience of eating – seeing the colours, smelling the aromas, feeling the textures and savouring the taste – while listening to the soft sounds of conversation around me.

During these breaks from conscious work, the back burner of my mind must have been simmering, because when I returned to my desk, new ideas and insights came with greater ease. By softening the focus, stretching time and releasing any sense of urgency, I found a door to discovery that had not been apparent previously. I engaged in the kind of thinking we do when the pressure's off, which tends to be more intuitive and creative. Maybe it's why Albert Einstein spent hours staring into space while he conducted his open-ended 'what if' experiments of the free-thinking mind.

Just as I had learned to enter the present moment through the senses, to step into the here and now through walking and to let go of the things and activities that fragment one's energy and attention, I was now learning how to live in the heart of work – loving the process as much as the product, the questions as much as the answers, the unknown as much as the known.

In the past, my busy schedule had been governed by a long 'to-do' list, and I was striving to 'get it all done'. Now, I was horrified by the thought. What does it mean to 'get it all done'? What a terrible day that would be. Then what? I realised that, ever so subtly, I had shifted gears in my life and my work. Now, the purpose and indeed the pleasure lay in the doing, enjoying the work and the interludes equally, aware that everything was part of a larger, seamless process. I was starting to sense what physicist Richard Feynman described when he said, 'The prize is the pleasure of finding the thing out, the kick in the discovery, the observation that other people use it – those are the real things.'

And there was more: not only did I gain an enormous pleasure from being immersed in work that mattered to me – I was excited about it! I began to trust the process and let go of the need to direct it or control it. I followed the path as it arose, starting with one research source and following the leads as they appeared, playing with ideas and asking 'what if' to test the range of possibility. By being completely present in my work, I was confident that this was the only thing I could be doing in this moment and that the path I was following was good. In a way, I could do no wrong. There could be no such thing as a mistake, because in making mistakes, I would learn and recalibrate and grow.

In following my instincts, I was bringing something – my writing – into existence. I was making concrete something that did not exist before. No matter how 'it' might turn out, the process of creation itself produces something that can never be wrong – engagement, meaning and aliveness. My little fragment of thinking might become something to touch and hold, and if it can help someone or inspire someone or simply entertain someone, that will be a bonus. The kick will have been in the doing.

'Thank you,' I said to the community of thinkers and writers through the centuries into whose line of enquiry I had stepped for a moment of insight and inspiration, and whose generous work helped me embrace the enormous pleasure of doing work I loved.

Happier here and now: bring the pleasure of doing what you love into your everyday life

Start with a simple tool*.* *To bring an activity you love into your life, start with a simple tool. If you want to be a writer, find an inspiring journal. If you want to be an artist, get a pocket-sized sketch pad to carry everywhere. To bring cooking back into your life, start with a beautiful piece of cookware. Use your new item the day you get it. And the next day. And every day after that. This simple item can become a talisman of your commitment to do what you love.*

Take a class*.* *There is no better way to kickstart yourself into doing what you love. Not only do you learn your craft and improve your skills, but you join a community of fellow practitioners. Sometimes that means sharing tips and techniques; often, it simply means working alongside those who share a love for this particular craft. A class boosts your motivation and accountability. You might surprise yourself with what you can do!*

Learn about people in your field*.* *Another way to deepen your connection to an activity you love is to learn more about other practitioners of the craft – past and present. What inspired them? How did they do their work? In what ways might you walk in their shoes and try their methods? Not only will you grow as a practitioner – you'll start to see and feel your own place in the history and tapestry of this work. There is no part too small!*

6

The Pleasure of Appreciation

Languedoc, France, 2015

After a few days at La Muse, I got sick. I curled up in bed and shivered under a massive pile of blankets. The weather turned cold and damp. Smells wafting up from the kitchen made me feel queasy. All the beautiful French food I had bought . . . I told my friends at the house to eat it, please.

It took time, but slowly I got better. On the fifth morning, I had enough energy to walk through the village. After, I used leftover vegetables to make soup. When it was ready, I filled a big ceramic bowl and carried it to the table. I dropped ragged pieces of stale baguette into the soup and loved the taste of the soggy crusts. I'd been so alive when I got here, bursting with creative inspiration. Then, I'd been incapacitated. Feeling my strength return, I was grateful for simple things like energy and an appetite.

I sat at my desk, and the flow of ideas became a torrent! I worked quickly, to capture the insights before they flew away. Later, I realised that the days spent under the covers constituted time and space where ideas could float and form without pressure, into a creative surge. I could see value now in both the wellness and the illness . . .

London, December 2013

The calendar continued to shed its pages, and I fell into a comfortable routine – waking early in my small room, listening to the rumble of the commuter trains, sipping hot coffee and eating warm oatmeal with the pop of fresh blueberries. Most mornings, I walked to the British Library, where I continued to read, write, think and sit happily among like-minded colleagues. Some evenings, I'd meet my son for a casual supper, or see one of my London friends for a drink at the pub; others, I'd return to my room for a bowl of soup and a good book. I felt a growing sense of peace. The worries and fears that had plagued me visited less often. If I got stuck in a loop of rumination, I used my new strategies to break free: The five senses brought me into the moment. While walking, I used my mantra of *here, now, here, now* in a rhythm that matched my steps. The fact that I had few possessions and even fewer obligations lent an ease to daily life. I was excited about my work. Most of the time, I was present in the moment, and life felt simply and tentatively good.

Then, 21 December popped up in the calendar. It was time to leave Primrose Hill and move to Highgate in north London. I'd planned with my Canadian friends, Jason and Karen, to swap flats. They needed to go home to Toronto for Christmas, and we figured they could stay in my place there while I stayed in theirs. We'd all have accommodation for the holidays, with the added security of knowing someone was taking care of things.

Getting ready to leave my perfect spot in Primrose Hill made me feel nostalgic. It had been a haven of simplicity, a place that asked nothing yet supported me in an uncluttered, cosy cocoon. I was leaving a refuge and stepping back into the bigger sphere of life. I was also moving one step closer to 'real life' back in Canada. I hadn't expected to feel so nervous.

By late afternoon I was ready. I opened the door of my room and ventured into the larger apartment where my host Sara lived with her two daughters. I poked my head into the living room and was surprised to see their Christmas tree, white lights twinkling in the descending dusk. I hadn't been thinking much about Christmas.

'Sara?' I called. 'Are you home?'

'I'm here, honey,' said Sara as she came out of the kitchen, wiping her hands on an apron. 'Are you off?'

'Yes, I am,' I said, 'I just wanted to say thank you for everything.'

'Thank you,' said Sara and she gave me a big hug. 'Make sure you come to stay with us again.'

'Don't worry,' I said. 'This feels like home to me. I mean it!'

Sara helped me carry my bags outside and a cab pulled up moments later. We hugged again while the driver loaded my things into the cavernous back seat.

'Goodbye! Come back soon! And, Merry Christmas!' Sara called as the car pulled away.

'You too!' I said and waved. I sat back and watched the townhouses of Primrose Hill go by in a pastel blur, now alight with Christmas decorations. My first Christmas as a newly single woman. Sara never knew me as the married person I was for most of my adult life. She had no idea that this time last year I lived in a beautiful house overlooking a ravine, with a massive stone fireplace that would be glowing every night. She didn't know how I loved sitting in front of that fire, curled up in the overstuffed chair, with our Labrador Retriever at my feet and our fat orange cat nestled beside me. She didn't know me when I had a husband who whistled 'Walking in a winter wonderland . . .' while he threaded Christmas lights through the shrubs outside before he hauled the Christmas tree inside and wrestled it into the stand in the corner. A year ago, I would have finished baking dozens of cookies – shortbread, almond, chocolate chip and Stuart's favourite, ginger creams. The freezer would be full of home-made sausage patties, fragrant meat pies and flaky butterscotch buns. I'd have decorated, planned our annual holiday open house and wrapped the gifts.

But – that was the old me. The new me hadn't done anything like that. Somehow the clock had sped up and Christmas was landing on my doorstep with a thud.

'Here we are, miss!' The cabbie pulled up in front of Jason and Karen's flat.

Miss . . .? Right. Well, he is right.

'Thanks very much,' I said and handed him the fare. 'Oh . . . and Merry Christmas,' I said as I pulled my bags from the back seat.

'You too!' he said. He smiled and drove away.

I stood at the front door and thought I'd take a minute to centre myself. Deep breath in . . . 'Fragrant,' I said to myself as I inhaled the crisp scent from the big cedar wreath. 'Crystal clear,' I said as I heard the bright sound of bells coming from the nearby church. 'Shiny,' I said as I looked at the freshly painted door in front of me. At that moment, the door swung open.

'Welcome and come on in!' said Karen as she reached for my bag and pulled me inside at the same time.

'Welcome and Merry Christmas,' said Jason as he came forward carrying their suitcases. 'We're like ships in the night!' he said.

'Our airport taxi comes in half an hour,' said Karen. 'That gives us just enough time for a little Christmas cheer!'

We sat down in the living room, and I looked around. A real spruce tree was laden with Christmas decorations and scented candles covered every flat surface.

'Wow. Your place looks beautiful,' I said, feeling overwhelmed.

'We enjoyed putting up all the decorations, and now you can relax and enjoy the season,' said Karen. 'Besides, we wanted you to have a real Christmas. You know—'

Jason interrupted. 'Just have fun. Make yourself at home. Eat and drink whatever you can find. And, did I say have fun?' He winked and poured each of us a glass of red wine.

I smiled and raised my glass. 'Here's to new beginnings. And to Christmas. And to my good fortune, spending the holidays in your beautiful home!'

'Merry Christmas!' we chimed as we clinked our glasses. Not long after that, their driver rang at the front door. Jason and Karen pulled on their coats, picked up their bags and left. I caught a whiff of cedar as the freshly painted door closed behind them.

I spent the rest of the evening drifting around their flat. The elegant two-storey space seemed huge in comparison to my little bed-sitting room in Primrose Hill. The gorgeous gourmet kitchen was equipped with everything one could want and more. I went upstairs to the beautiful master bedroom with its adjacent bath and dressing room. I unpacked and poured myself a glass of wine. I wandered over to the Christmas tree to examine their decorations up close. Fingering the sweet ornaments – small silver sleighs, miniature bells, a tiny gingerbread man – my mind went to Christmases past, at home with Stuart and Ryan. Through the years, we had created many traditions. This very day, the Saturday before Christmas, Stuart would put up the tree, I'd string it with lights and Ryan would hang the decorations, a crazy collection of bits and pieces amassed through the years. We'd loop fresh cedar rope up the banister and along the railing of the gallery overlooking the great room. Afterward, we'd toast the season with Brandy Alexanders made using my grandfather's recipe. On Christmas Eve, we'd invite friends and neighbours in for drinks and a buffet supper. The three of us always spent Christmas morning in front of the fireplace, taking forever to open our stockings and gifts while enjoying a long, unhurried breakfast.

Last December, Stuart and I had visited Ryan in London, because he couldn't make it home to Canada for the holidays. Then, a few weeks later, Stuart and I had our first Christmas at home without Ryan – just the two of us. We followed our family traditions and enjoyed a long, lazy day with the dog and the cat and each other. Our first 'empty nest' Christmas had seemed relaxed and easy.

And now? I was in a lovely home, tastefully decorated for the holidays, sipping wine and listening to beautiful music. And I felt more alone than I had in weeks.

'What am I doing here?' Isolation swirled around me. I was painfully aware of Stuart's absence and even more acutely aware of his choice. Was he sitting in front of the fire with her now? Was he stealing a warm cookie from the tray she'd just taken from the oven? What did she think as she unpacked the lumpy clay Christmas decorations Ryan made when he was in kindergarten? Did they even make it onto the tree?

The only thing I knew for sure was that Stuart wasn't here in my life. It was the same feeling I had in the days and months after my mom died. *Not here, still not here . . . and finally sinking in: never here again.* Tears filled my eyes. The flickering candles and twinkling tree lights became a bright blur. I stepped back and fell sideways onto an overstuffed ottoman. Righting myself, I sat down and held my tear-soaked face in my hands. I remembered what the writer Julian Barnes said after the death of his wife, 'All couples, even the most bohemian, build up patterns in their lives together, and these patterns have an annual cycle. So Year One is like a negative image of the year you have been used to. Instead of being studded with events, it is now studded with non-events . . .'

I had just lurched into my first non-event, the first Christmas without the man who had been my partner for decades.

Panic crept up my spine. I felt dizzy. This was like the fear I had when my dad died – that feeling of dread when you're alone in unfamiliar territory, with no one to catch you should you fall. Staying very still and keeping my head down, I peered through my fingers. I needed to focus on something tangible. 'Paisley,' I said out loud as my eyes fell on the fabric covering the ottoman. 'Vanilla,' I said as the scent reached me from the candle on the coffee table. 'Sweet,' I said, hearing the strains of a boys' choir singing 'O Tannenbaum' on the radio.

Connecting to the senses steadied me. But I still felt alone and afraid. I blew out the candles, switched off the lights and climbed the stairs to bed. I pulled the comforter over my head and fell asleep.

* * *

I woke early the next morning and made my way down to the kitchen. Dawn's first light peeked between the slats of the window shutters, portending an uncharacteristically bright morning in London. I moved with care. I didn't want to dislodge the emotions that had overwhelmed me the night before. I padded over to the sink to fill the kettle.

I sat down at the kitchen table and ran my hand across its rough surface. Jason and Karen liked to mix rustic pieces of furniture with more elegant, classic items. It worked. This sturdy wooden table felt reassuring. A gentle sadness filled me. Today the feeling was softer, more wistful. My hand moved across the table, sensing smooth then rough then smooth again. I let the feelings in.

'There's sadness,' I said. 'Hello, old friend.'

'And worry,' I noticed. 'I know you well.'

'Warm,' I said, filling my coffee mug.

'And light,' I said as I gathered the courage to open the blinds fully. 'Beautiful sunshine.'

I sat back down at the table and sipped my coffee. I

let the feelings, thoughts and sensations come and go, rise and fall, with my breathing.

As the morning progressed I moved like someone recovering from a fall, still bruised and sore but knowing it was better to work through the discomfort than resist it. The pain and panic from the night before had subsided. 'Remember,' I reminded myself. 'Feelings, thoughts, events – good and bad, in equal measure – are going to come and go. Nothing lasts for ever.'

To chase only the 'good' feelings while resisting the 'bad' would be to embrace half a life, the supposed good half, while struggling to squirm away from the other half. That didn't make sense. I thought about poet Rainer Maria Rilke's advice to a young writer: 'Let everything happen to you: beauty and terror. Just keep going. No feeling is final.'

'Right,' I thought. No feeling is final. In fact, nothing is for ever. Neither the good nor the bad. Rather than trying to make one thing last or another thing end, why not allow it all, knowing it will rise and fall in its own rhythm anyway? Wasn't this what I had been experiencing in the last few weeks? Being present, loving the here and now, letting go and allowing life to unfold in the moment?

Even in sadness, I wanted to be here for what was happening now – for the beauty, and the terror. In a line from *Hamlet*, Shakespeare said, 'there is nothing either good or bad, but thinking makes it so.' In other words, events, and even thoughts and feelings, are not innately anything at all. They acquire negative and positive value only when we label them. If we don't label them, they lose their power, and we are less likely to suffer. I could see now that I had been operating with an implicit assumption: that if I got through the pain and sadness, I would reach a better, brighter place. What if this pain and sadness were worth much more than that – not something to endure but something to embrace?

What if I didn't label or resist any of it, and allowed all of it, with genuine gratitude? I thought about what had happened in the last year and particularly in the last two months. There was a silver lining: I had been given the freedom and flexibility to live in the incredible city of London. I got to spend time with my son, seeing him happy and working, in daily life. I was free of the obligations and commitments that had stolen my creative time in the past. And I was becoming reacquainted with myself – rediscovering parts that had been suppressed for years and finding new aspects that were springing up through the cracks.

I sat back down at the wooden table. I ran my fingers over the rough sections and the smooth parts and saw that both were needed to make the table not only whole but beautiful. It was all one thing, and it was perfect.

I decided to do some errands. Ryan would be coming to stay from Christmas Eve to Boxing Day, and I wanted to get things ready. I thought about the notion of gratitude for everything, not just for what we deemed to be good things. What would happen if I managed to appreciate everything, in every moment, as it happened?

I took the tube to Oxford Street, where classic

British department stores sat sandwiched among the world's ubiquitous retail chains. With only three days to go before Christmas, it seemed half of London's population and all its million tourists had flocked to the same street. By the time I arrived, the early morning sunshine was nowhere to be seen. The day had turned cold and grey, and dampness had settled into every corner. I shivered. Then, the rain started. I hadn't brought an umbrella, and I needed to traverse about a dozen blocks of Oxford Street. I joined the crowd. A woman came up behind me on the right, pushing a buggy festooned with overstuffed shopping bags. I stepped left to let her pass, and my foot caught the edge of the kerb. Going over on my ankle, I fell on my hands and knees, into the street. I looked up to see a cyclist swerve around me at the last minute. 'Lucky that's all there was,' I thought as I scrambled back onto the sidewalk. Now hobbling on my sore ankle, I tried to keep pace with the surge of people. As I was being jostled along while getting soaked by the rain, I couldn't help but feel alone in the crowd.

I caught my reflection in a shop window. Looking back at me was a small figure, skinny legs sticking out from a shapeless coat, fine wet hair plastered over her brow. Is she slightly bent over, or tired, or is she just getting old? I turned away from the window and reached behind my head for the hood of my coat. I needed to hide or, better yet, disappear. I pulled up the hood, and all the rain it had collected over the past several blocks now trickled neatly down the middle of my back.

'Screw this,' I said under my breath. I leaned against the window and stood there. I wanted to go home. Not to Jason and Karen's glamorous flat but to my small safe room in Primrose Hill. I wanted to get into bed and listen to the trains. Maybe make some tea or have a bath. I stood frozen under the awning, cold and wet, watching people go by. I thought about my morning resolve to reach for gratitude, no matter what. *Right. Well, I'm not feeling it. I don't want to do it.*

'Even more reason then,' I said. I didn't want to do it, but I stepped back into the stream of people. I put one foot in front of the other.

'Right now, I get to visit one of the most famous, iconic streets in the world,' I thought.

The rain continued, and I got wetter.

'Right now, I get to feel the rain fall. Not loving it, but it's not killing me. I can't get any wetter than I already am.'

I kept walking. I was pushed around a bit, but when I met other people's eyes we exchanged smiles.

'Right now, I get to be with people from every country and every corner of life.'

I spotted the first shop on my list and went in.

'Right now, I get to buy gifts for my son, with whom I will spend Christmas,' I thought. I bought the usual socks and underwear for his Christmas stocking. Back outside the shop, I saw a dishevelled young man who looked like he had camped on the cold, wet street all night. His frayed cap sat upturned in front of him. I emptied my pocket into the cap.

'Bless you,' he said.

'Merry Christmas,' I said.

I finished shopping and headed to Oxford Circus

tube. The queue for the escalator was long, so I took the stairs.

'Right now, I get to enjoy reasonably good health. And I'm pretty sure I didn't break my ankle.' I rode the tube to Highgate station and walked back to the flat. The rain had stopped, and the sun was trying to push its way back out from behind the clouds.

I unpacked the gifts I'd bought for Ryan and laid them out on the couch. 'Perfect,' I thought. I was looking forward to Christmas Eve. I changed into dry clothes, made a fire and sat down with a cup of tea. I wasn't lamenting a day spent in the rain and the crowds. My experiment might have made a difference. If nothing else, the damp and the wet and the throngs provided a contrast to the warmth and peacefulness that now enveloped me. Instead of pronouncing things bad or good, and then resisting the so-called bad, I found a way to move through it. I needed practice, but I could sense a shift. I liked what writer Thomas Wolfe said in a letter to his mother: 'It is not all bad, but it is not all good, it is not all ugly, but it is not all beautiful, it is life, life, life – the only thing that matters.'

There is nothing either good or bad, but thinking makes it so. To be grateful for all of it was to be grateful for life. Simple. And yet, why didn't it come more naturally? I decided to continue my appreciation experiments. I'd see if author Sarah Ban Breathnach was right when she said, 'Gratitude bestows reverence, allowing us to encounter everyday epiphanies, those transcendent moments of awe that change for ever how we experience life and the world.'

Over the next couple of days, I reflected on the meaning of gratitude. The word is from the Latin 'gratia' for grace, graciousness and gratefulness. The link between gratitude and grace appealed to me. To me, 'grace' embodied elegance and ease. It required a lightness of touch, and a letting go of the desire to make things a certain way. To allow and appreciate whatever was happening, free of wanting things to be any other way.

Living in gratitude meant living in freedom, in grace, in ease and in full.

I went back to the question of why gratitude seemed so elusive when the benefits seemed so clear. How might I appreciate life more readily? Maybe the answer lay in appreciating death as well.

Cultures through the ages have shone the light on death. The logic made sense: the more we are aware of death, the more we cherish everything life gives us. There is not only an appreciation of life, but an urgency to live with gusto. When physician and writer Oliver Sacks faced terminal brain cancer, he wrote, 'I feel a sudden clear focus and perspective . . . I feel intensely alive, and I want and hope in the time that remains to deepen my friendships, to say farewell to those I love, to write more, to travel if I have the strength, to achieve new levels of understanding and insight.'

I had seen death close up and experienced its impact on those left behind. I was all too aware of how much life my parents had missed. They didn't see us graduate from college. They didn't get to hold their grandchildren or potter in retirement. My mom would have done even more painting and sewing. She would have adored her seven grandkids and marvelled at her five great-grandsons. My dad might have built that fishing cabin he'd always wanted. My parents missed life, literally. Now, I needed to be sure I didn't miss it by dancing around the bits I didn't like; or by pushing blindly through one so-called busy day after another; or by taking small, everyday pleasures for granted.

Oliver Sacks said, 'I cannot pretend I am without fear. But my predominant feeling is one of gratitude. I have loved and been loved; I have been given much and I have given something in return; I have read and travelled and thought and written . . . Above all, I have been a sentient being, a thinking animal, on this beautiful planet, and that, in itself, has been an enormous privilege and adventure.'

I figured if I could have gratitude for life now, as it happened, moment by moment, I might have a better chance of experiencing all of 'life, life, life – the only thing that matters'.

Christmas Eve arrived. At six o'clock there was a knock, and I opened the door. Ryan came in laden with his overnight bag, shopping and parcels. He hugged me and made his way to the kitchen to unpack the groceries.

'I bought us a chicken for tonight. We can do it the

way we like, with lemons and garlic. And I'm going to try my new scrambled eggs on Christmas morning. I'm copying the way they make them at the Dorchester Hotel. I think I've got the method down, but I want to know what you think. I also brought some wine that I think you'll find interesting . . . Is there a corkscrew?'

'In the drawer to your right, Ryan,' I said. 'I love all your ideas. Are you sure you're okay not doing all the things we used to do at Christmas?'

'Maybe it's time for some new traditions,' he said. He handed me a glass of wine. 'Merry Christmas, Mum.'

'Merry Christmas, Ryan,' I said. 'Here's to new traditions.' We clinked our glasses and took a sip.

'Mmm, that's good,' said Ryan. Turning back to the kitchen counter, he pulled down a cutting board, reached for a knife and began slicing lemons. He started to hum, 'Walking in a winter wonderland . . .'

Past, present, here, there . . . it melded together in one beautiful moment of life.

'Right now, I get to be with my wonderful son on Christmas Eve,' I said out loud. Ryan laughed. I joined him in the kitchen and started peeling garlic.

Happier here and now: bring the pleasure of appreciation into your everyday life

Practice just-in-time gratitude by saying, 'Right now, I get to . . .'. *The most powerful experience of gratitude happens when you link it to what is happening right now. Several times a day, pause briefly to say, 'Right now, I get to . . .' and describe three very specific, tangible things you appreciate in this very moment. This can be especially helpful if you are feeling down or if things don't seem to be going well. There's still a way to see what's good in the moment.*

Pop on the rose-coloured glasses. *Think of a condition, event or person in your life right now that you are resisting, disliking, or pushing away. Now, list three things about that condition, event or person for which you can feel grateful. The 'silver lining' if you will.*

Conduct a gratitude inventory. *What do you appreciate most about your body? What about your brain? What aspect of your personality has been most helpful to you lately? In what ways are you grateful for each member of your family? Your closest friends? What aspect of your immediate environment causes you to feel grateful? Be specific. Add your own questions. Make it current, take a broad view, and keep a running list.*

7
The Pleasure of Connection

Languedoc, France, 2015

At La Muse, we fell into the habit of sharing our food. When I first arrived, John and Kerry showed me to my corner of the fridge and cupboards. In the morning, I'd come downstairs to make coffee and toast, which I carried back to my room so as not to waste a moment of precious writing time. The others there were similar, especially during the day. We'd run into one another on the stairs or in the kitchen, but we were respectful of each other's mental and creative space. It was not the time for conversation beyond a pleasant hello or how's it going.

By five o'clock, the light softened, and the energy shifted. One evening, I came down to the kitchen to find Lynn and Gillian chopping onions and garlic, sipping wine and laughing.

'Please, join us,' said Gillian as she splashed some red wine into a short glass.

'Thanks!' I said, appreciative of the camaraderie. From my part of the fridge, I pulled out a tub of fat green olives

and dumped them into a shallow bowl. 'Please,' I said as I extended the bowl to them.

Before long, we were throwing a bit of everything from our collective stores into the pot. Without a plan, we produced a rich, red pasta sauce with earthy mushrooms, shiny peppers and bright green basil. Adrian and Ellie joined us.

'Sorry, all I've got left is stale bread,' said Adrian. 'But it's great toasted with olive oil and garlic.' He got down one of the long wooden boards and sawed through his bread lengthwise.

'I'll set the table,' said Ellie.

Half an hour later, we were seated in the white-plastered, low-ceilinged dining room, sharing a meal of pasta, garlicky bread and salad from chipped and mismatched ceramic bowls. A bottle of local wine sat open, and we poured it into an array of glasses and cups.

'Cheers!' we said as we raised our glasses.

'May the muse smile on us!' I said, happy for the effortless ease of friendship discovered in that moment.

Happier Here and Now

London, December 2013

It arrived: the first Christmas morning of this new unasked-for chapter of our lives. I woke early and peered out the window at a typical London winter's day – cold, damp and grey. Shivering, I dressed quickly in thick socks, jeans and a big sweater over a long-sleeved T-shirt. I still wasn't used to draughty British flats.

From the top of the stairs, I smelled coffee and heard the snap of wood burning in the fireplace. As I descended, I saw Ryan sitting on the couch, leaning forward and staring into the fire. He held a steaming mug of coffee in two hands. Was he thinking of the long, lazy Christmas mornings we'd spent as a family, gathered around the big stone fireplace to eat breakfast and open gifts? Did he miss his dad?

'Merry Christmas, Ryan.' I walked behind him and put my hand on his shoulder.

'Merry Christmas, Mum,' he said. 'I was just thinking about how Henry liked to lie on the warm stone in front of the fire.'

I was right. Ryan's thoughts were of our home, all of us together, even the dog and cat.

'Yeah, Henry was something, wasn't he?' Our big brown dog would lie there, getting unbelievably hot, and yet he still wouldn't move. He was only eleven when he died suddenly last July. 'I miss him too, Ryan. He'd be right in front of the fire today, for sure. Well, Sammy's still there,' I added. 'I'm sure he misses you.'

'Do you think so?' Ryan asked. 'I wonder if dogs and cats miss people.'

'I think they do,' I said. 'Not that they know it's Christmas. But we do, don't we?'

'Yeah,' said Ryan. 'This is different. But it's okay.'

'I know. And it's strange without your dad, right? I thought you might give him a call this afternoon when the time zones line up. I'm thinking of going for a walk then anyway,' I said.

'Sounds good,' said Ryan. 'And, we've got company tonight. That'll be fun.'

Ryan had made lots of friends during his two years in London. They were an international bunch, and many couldn't make it home for Christmas. We'd invited a few of them over, to share a Christmas meal together. It seemed like a good call. We'd both appreciate the distraction.

'I'm looking forward to it,' I said.

'Me too,' said Ryan. He stood up and stretched. 'Are you hungry? If you are, I'm ready to start the eggs.'

'Let's do it!' I said, and we headed for the kitchen.

Ryan made the scrambled eggs, and they were rich and decadently creamy. We had thick rashers of bacon and fat slices of crusty white toast, slathered with butter and strawberry jam. We ate breakfast in front of the fire, just like at home, while laughing over the funny little gifts we'd sneaked into each other's Christmas stockings. The morning passed quietly and pleasantly. Ryan stoked the fire and lazed on the couch, thumbing through the books I'd given him. I read the January edition of *Vogue* that Ryan always put into my stocking (this time it was British *Vogue*), and checked my horoscope for the coming year. I caught myself hoping for a better year, but then realised I didn't have a clue what that might look like. 'Besides, what's the point,' I thought. I'd learned that time spent in the future was likely to be full of worry and anxiety. Who needed that?

'Right now, I'm with my son on Christmas morning. We're safe and healthy, and enjoying the day,' I thought, and smiled to myself. I went into the kitchen to do the dishes and poke around at what we'd be cooking for dinner.

Just after noon, I got ready to head out.

'I'm going for a walk, Ryan,' I said in the direction of the couch and fireplace.

Ryan's head popped up from behind the back of the couch. It looked like he'd been dozing.

'Okay, Mum. Have a good walk.'

'And you're going to call your dad, right?'

'Yep. I'll get my laptop now,' he said.

'Say Merry Christmas from me.' I didn't want to talk to Stuart, but there was no reason not to wish him well. For Ryan's sake, as much as mine.

'Will do!' said Ryan.

I went out and headed down the road from Jason and Karen's flat, skirting the village of Highgate on the way to Hampstead Heath. The streets were quiet, but chimneys were puffing out fragrant smoke. Christmas tree lights glowed from behind steamy windows. Homes grew larger and more elegant as I passed through the affluent Grove district. I continued my descent down Highgate Hill and entered the heath from Merton Lane. I started along one of many paths, and it became apparent that a walk on the heath was a popular Christmas afternoon pastime. It seemed that all those who weren't tucked into cosy houses were out for an afternoon stroll. Families, older couples, joggers and dogs – it was busier than I'd ever seen it. I quickened my pace, to get the blood moving against the chill that hung in the damp air and to shake off the sadness that started to seep in when I saw families walking together.

Unlike stately Regent's Park with its gorgeous gardens or pretty Primrose Hill Park with its expansive playing fields, Hampstead Heath was a huge nature reserve, covering almost eight hundred acres. I walked without a plan, finding myself on dirt paths that had been trodden into place through the years. Moving from open fields to wooded thickets and back into the open again, I exchanged Christmas greetings and smiles with those I passed. The brisk walk was helping me shake the chill, but not the sadness. I felt terrible for Ryan, who'd lost his family. Was it as different for him now as it had been for me decades ago, when my family shattered apart after my dad died? Granted, Ryan had never known what it was like to have siblings, but he did grow up in a happy home. Even though he'd moved to London, I was sure he had liked the idea that his mom and dad went about their lives in the house he'd known in the town where he grew up back in Canada. A place where he could return to find the unbroken line of his life story.

But it did break. And it would stay broken, for ever. Just a year ago, I was happily clueless about what was about to happen. I thought my story of loss was safely entrenched in the past, that I'd created a stable life for my family. When the cracks appeared in January, I believed they could be repaired. When the split came in May, I thought it was a test – a big test – that Stuart and I would pass before we got back together, stronger than ever. When I came to London in June to tell Ryan, I wove a shred of hope into the story because I believed it was there. Now, enough time had passed, more than enough truth had emerged and Christmas had arrived to put it all into sharp, shiny focus.

The path I was following split into three strands. Rather than choose one, I elected to sit on a bench tucked into a treed alcove. A large, extended family rambled by. Grandpa was using his walking stick to point out various plants to the kids; Grandma held his other arm and laughed as she spoke with the attractive woman who walked beside her. They shared the same petite build and fair hair. Mother and daughter, I presumed. The younger woman looked about ten years my junior, and I assumed the lanky man walking behind them was her husband. One of the twenty-somethings carried a tiny bundle in a cloth baby-carrier against her chest. Did that make four generations?

As I watched them walk across the heath, I became aware of an unsettled feeling.

'There's envy,' I thought. Then, a soft pain . . . 'And sadness.'

I let the feelings in and allowed my attention to widen. A fat beagle came over the hill, sniffing right and left. I inhaled too.

'Musty.' I picked up the smell of the leaves all around me, slowly decomposing into the mulch that would feed the flowers come spring.

The beagle trotted, nose down, to investigate the pile of leaves next to my bench. He poked and prodded, then looked up at me. He sat down and wagged his tail, as though I'd been the goal of his search all along,

'Hey, buddy,' I said, leaning down to pat the dog. His velvety ears were cold. I rubbed them, and the dog closed his eyes. He reminded me of my childhood dog Nicky, also a beagle. Then, I thought of our beautiful dog Henry. It had been only a few weeks after I moved into my little apartment in Toronto last summer when Stuart called me.

'It's Henry,' he said. 'He collapsed this morning, and I took him to the vet. He's there now, and they're doing tests.'

I jumped in the car, raced to my old home town and went straight to the vet's office. Henry was in a big cage at floor level. I sat down and said his name. Through eyes glazed with painkillers, he looked at me, and the end of his tail flicked back and forth. The vet put a blanket on the floor and opened the cage door. Henry stumbled out and lay down with his head in my lap. I stroked his head, and we stayed like that for a long while. Stuart arrived and sat down with us. Soon after that, the vet came in.

'The tests are back,' she said. 'It looks like he's got a tumour at the base of his brain. It's too far gone for surgery. And he was in an enormous amount of pain before we sedated him. It's not something he can live with. I'm sorry.'

'What do you mean?' I asked.

'The kindest thing would be to put him down.'

Stuart's face crumpled, and he put his head in both hands. I heard the quiet sobs. Tears ran down my cheeks. Stuart moved closer and put one arm around my shoulder. He rested his other hand on Henry's head.

'Well . . .?' The vet looked at us, and we nodded. She left the room, to give us time with Henry. I lay on the blanket with my arms tightly around his neck and my face buried in his warm coat. Stuart kept one hand on my shoulder and the other on Henry. A little later, the vet returned with the needle and told us we could stay there on the floor with him.

'Goodbye, buddy,' I said, with my arms tightly encircling our big, warm dog. 'We love you. Thank you.'

We held Henry as she slowly injected the serum. One minute, I could feel him alive under my touch. And then, he was gone. There was a dog's body on the blanket, but Henry was no longer present. Stuart stood up, his face soaked with tears.

'I'm sorry,' he said. 'I have to go home. See you there?'

I nodded yes.

'We can take things from here,' said the vet. I thanked her, but I couldn't bring myself to leave. I don't know how long it was before I managed to lift Henry's head from my lap and let it rest softly on the blanket. I took the other end of the blanket and covered Henry up to his chin, trying to make him more comfortable even though I knew he was dead. I walked to the car in a daze and drove back to the house that was no longer my home. Stuart was sitting on the front steps. I sat beside him.

'I can't believe it,' we took turns saying. 'It's impossible,' we said. 'He's gone.'

We sat beside each other and cried.

And then I felt tears, but I was back on Hampstead Heath. I was patting the beagle with my eyes closed, and I was crying. I missed Henry. I missed Stuart. I missed our home and our life as a family. Everything I'd been doing the last two months – being present, losing myself in work, practising gratitude, living through the senses – it was helping. I was learning what it felt like to let go and stay in the moment and watch the sorrows and the joys rise and fall. The hard edges of pain had softened, and the constant whirr of hamster-wheel thinking had virtually stopped. Yet, there were still times when sadness and grief landed heavily. I missed the man who'd been my husband, lover and friend. In our twenty-five years together, I hadn't held anything back, no reservations. Should I have cordoned off a corner of my heart, just in case? But then I'd have missed the fullness of the love we did have.

I took a deep breath and opened my eyes. They met the brown eyes of the little beagle, who was still sitting at my feet, regarding me with friendly curiosity. I looked over his head at the faded greens and browns of the English winter foliage. I imagined the transformation that would come in a few months, as these reticent hues would give way to the bright, boisterous tones of spring. I trusted this would happen, even though there was no sign of it today. 'Maybe I'm in a winter of my own', I thought. 'What had been unreserved love, in full colour, has gone. Despite the loss, life continues, and something will emerge. I'd been hoping I could hurry things along, but I now realised that this too would evolve at its own speed.

The poet David Whyte says, 'We use the word *heartbreak* as if it only occurs when things have gone wrong: an unrequited love, a shattered dream ...

But heartbreak may be the very essence of being human, of being on the journey from here to there, and of coming to care deeply for what we find along the way.'

'Maggie! Here, Maggie!'

A rumpled chap who looked to be in his seventies came along one of the three paths that converged across from my bench. His brown corduroy trousers bagged at the knees, and his boots were covered in mud. The beagle's head turned, and she shot toward him.

'There you are!' he said. The dog fell in beside him and trotted along. He caught my eye. 'She's a scamp,' he said. 'Always running miles ahead, following her nose wherever it goes.'

'Well, I enjoyed visiting with her,' I said. 'She's sweet. Reminds me of my dog.'

'Oh, that's nice,' he said. 'Yes, she's good company. Aren't you?' He reached down and ruffled her ears. 'Well, I'd best get home. There's a turkey pie in the oven that'll be ready in fifteen minutes. Merry Christmas!'

'Merry Christmas!' I said to the gentleman and his beagle. They headed off and disappeared over the hill.

I imagined him arriving home, leaving his muddy boots by the door and retrieving his slippers, before padding into the kitchen to take his dinner from the oven. Perhaps he was recently widowed, and would sit at the table, all too aware of the empty spot across from him. Maybe he'd raise a glass and make a silent toast to her and the happy years they shared. Then, he'd reach down to pat the dog and lean forward to catch the fragrant aroma of the hot turkey pie.

'Hi, Ryan,' I called as I arrived back at the flat. Delicious smells filled the air.

'Hi, Mum,' said Ryan as he came around the corner, drying his hands on a tea towel he'd tucked into his jeans. 'I thought I'd get a head start on the cooking.'

'Thanks,' I said. 'It's great to come home to!' We walked into the kitchen, where Ryan had bacon, shallots, garlic and mushrooms sizzling together in a red-enamelled cast-iron pot. 'Fantastic,' I said. 'Smells great, looks great and I know it will taste great!'

Ryan had already browned the meat. We were having beef bourguignon, our traditional family Christmas dinner. Stuart had always hated turkey, and we'd happened on a beef bourguignon recipe one Christmas. We'd tried it and loved it. Ryan and I thought it would be a good choice for his friends too.

'How was your call with Dad?' I asked.

'Fine,' said Ryan. 'Uncle Rob and Aunt Nora are staying with him. They were all just getting up.'

I was glad to hear that Stuart's brother and sister-in-law were visiting. I didn't need to know who else might be there.

'You're off to a great start here, Ryan,' I said. 'Just tell me what I can do.'

'Okay, if you open the wine, we can add that, combine everything and then it can go in the oven for a few hours. Easy!'

I opened the bottle of burgundy while Ryan returned the meat to the pan and added a few herbs. We splashed in some of the wine and turned up the heat to get all the brown bits from the bottom of the pan. Then he slowly tipped in the rest of the wine, placed the heavy lid on top and put the pot into the oven.

'*Voilà!*' he said.

'Fantastic,' I said. 'And thank you!'

While the stew simmered in the oven, Ryan went back to reading on the couch and stoking the fire. I pottered around the kitchen. I stood at the sink, scrubbing potatoes and letting the lukewarm water run over my hands. Looking out the window in the direction of the heath, I thought about my walk and the gentleman with the beagle. I couldn't know for sure, but he seemed to me like a man who'd been married most of his life. What was worse – losing someone after fifty years or after only twenty-five? Was the vacancy in his heart bigger than mine? Or did my pain, rooted not only in loss but in rejection by the man I loved, somehow come to match his? I remembered how alone my seven-year-old self had felt after my mother died, and how devastated and afraid I'd been after my father killed himself. In my life, loss had taken many different guises. Each experience was unique, yet all of them the same in one important way: they all ended in the permanent absence of someone I loved.

Our first response to the loss of a loved one is shock and disbelief. To us, it is literally as impossible to lose them as it would be to lose ourselves. Because in many ways we are losing a part of ourselves. The love and emotional energy we share feels as real as the air we breathe together. When the connection is broken, we are broken, our hearts are broken.

'Broken heart, open heart,' I mused.

After all, who doesn't understand what it feels like to have a broken heart? It made sense to me that we might connect with one another as much through loss as we would through love. From the place of our deepest pain, where we feel the loss of a specific connection, we might gain the capacity to make a more universal connection. In her memoir about recovery from addiction, Sarah Hepola says, 'When I listened to someone's story, when I met the eyes of a person in pain, I was lifted out of my own sadness, and the connection between us felt like a supernatural force I could not explain . . . I needed to be reminded I was not alone . . . I needed to be reminded that a human life is infinitesimal . . . that I am big and small at once.'

Big and small, whole and broken, alone and more connected than ever. If our very human brokenness is the soil from which new growth can arise, then it is, in a way, a gift. The leaves that were decomposing around me on the heath were not only bringing the next season's new growth to life; their scent brought the little beagle for a visit and her master the gentleman for a moment of human connection upon which I would reflect and gain new insights. Maybe the imperfection of today's conditions is what allows us to plant the seeds of tomorrow's growth. All the broken and open bits will let the light shine through and create new possibilities.

'Six for dinner, right?' I asked Ryan as I rummaged around for placemats and cutlery.

'Sean and Olivia, plus Matt, and Carl, and us. Yep, that makes six.'

I distributed everything around the table. I gathered

up a few candles and snipped a couple of small pine branches from the back of the Christmas tree. I popped them into a vase, and the table was ready.

Seven o'clock came and as though on cue, the doorbell rang.

'I'll get it!' said Ryan as he bounded to the front door and threw it open.

'Happy Christmas!' came a small chorus of voices. Our four guests arrived together, having shared a cab from central London up to Highgate. I took the tray of cheese puffs from the oven, slid them onto a platter and went out to greet everyone.

'Merry Christmas!' I said. 'Let us take your coats and then please come in and make yourselves comfortable.'

While Ryan gathered up their coats, I poured six glasses of English sparkling wine and distributed them to our guests.

'Happy Christmas!' said Olivia, and we all clinked our glasses.

'To Ryan and his mum,' said Carl. 'Thanks for having us. It's lovely to come to such a welcoming home on Christmas.'

'And we're happy to have you here,' I said. 'Now, let's sit down and enjoy the beautiful fire. Ryan's been keeping it going all day long!'

Sean and Olivia sat close together on the loveseat. Matt, Carl and Ryan took up spots on the sofas and ottoman. I pulled a chair over from the dining table. I listened as they shared stories of their holidays – Sean and Olivia were both English and were spending their first Christmas together since moving in together in the autumn. Olivia's parents had been divorced since she was little; Sean's parents were together, and his family planned to gather in the coming days. Matt was Irish and didn't have enough holiday time to go home for Christmas. He and his fiancée had split only a few weeks ago. Carl was from India and had a complicated family background – his parents were divorced and living in far-flung places. Ryan said it had been years since Carl had seen his father, who had started a new life with a new family. Carl had English godparents living not too far away, and he planned to see them soon.

All these friends met at the London School of Economics, where Ryan had first gone to study in the

UK. The group visiting us were a sample of the larger gang of friends he had collected during his time here so far. They were from all over the world, with a range of backgrounds and interests and stories.

Of the five young people, three, now including Ryan, had experienced their parents' break-up. One, Carl, saw his family only rarely and was estranged from his father. Matt had experienced the disappointment and sadness of the end of a once-promising relationship. Each of them had been visited by both joy and sorrow – as had I through my many more years.

Did I have any wisdom to impart today? I thought about Rainer Maria Rilke's advice to experience it all, the beauty and the terror, and Thomas Wolfe's letter saying, '. . . it is not all ugly, but it is not all beautiful, it is life, life, life – the only thing that matters.' Once, I thought I could protect my son from pain and sorrow. Now I could see that not only would that be impossible, it would also be wrong. Pain and sorrow were as much a part of an authentic life as joy and happiness. Love, loss and grief were amplified by the degree to which we were willing to experience life in full. Did I want to clip the corners of Ryan's experience, or have him do it, to achieve a false sense of security? Absolutely not. Nor did I want to clip my own, I realised. I looked at the optimistic, resilient young people in front of me and wished for them a full, exuberant life, the only thing that mattered.

'What better life could there be?' I thought.

A couple of hours later, we still lingered at the dinner table, sipping wine and chatting. The beef bourguignon had been a success. We'd finished the meal with flaky mince tarts and warm brandy cream.

Matt raised his glass. 'To friendship,' he said.

'To friendship,' we toasted.

I felt a warm connection with this little group. They were from all corners of the world, each with a unique story, much of which had yet to unfold. I was happy to know them, not only because they were part of the fabric of my son's life, but because we had shared this time and created an experience that each of us would carry forward. And more – we'd shown that we cared about one another.

Being kind and being present for the fullness of life. If I had to distil it, I'd say that's what I'd learned these past few months. I came to London seeking an escape, but I discovered a richer, fuller life in the process. I'd found paths to the present through the senses, through walking, by letting go, by doing good work, and through gratitude. And right now, I was grateful for the pain and sadness that had been my companions, because they were guiding me toward connection and kindness.

Facing the first Christmas of this new chapter in our lives, Ryan and I chose to open our home to friends, each with their own story of love, loss, joy and sorrow. The poet Naomi Shihab Nye says, 'Before you know kindness as the deepest thing inside, you must know sorrow as the other deepest thing . . . You must speak to it till your voice catches the thread of all sorrows and you see the size of the cloth.'

One cloth, six friends, around a wooden table, on Christmas. My grandmother's pearls felt cool against my skin and I was grateful for the string of moments that had brought me to this time and place. In that instant, I felt nothing could be more perfect than 'right here, right now'.

Happier here and now: bring the pleasure of connection into your everyday life

Identify what came through the cracks for you*.* *Think of a time when you lost someone or something that mattered – when your heart was broken. Then, think of three things that arose eventually as a result of that loss and your change in circumstances. This is not to say you would wish for that loss; only to highlight the good that managed to come through the cracks.*

Create a kindness habit*.* *It's easy to practice kindness every day. Every morning, identify a way to give something out of kindness, do something out of kindness, and say something out of kindness. That means at least three acts of kindness every day. They can be as small or as grand as you like. At the end of each day, jot down your acts of kindness. Take a minute to reflect on how you felt afterwards. Repeat the next day and the next. Soon, you'll be hooked on the power of kindness!*

Extend the hand of friendship*.* *Think of someone who has recently experienced loss, or who spends a lot of time alone, or who could simply use a kind word. Find a way to connect – in person, in writing, through a call, or a delivery of food or flowers. Reach out with a light touch to let them know they are in your thoughts. Do this with more people more often and you will weave a web of kindness that lifts everyone up.*

Epilogue

Languedoc, France, 2015

It was my second-to-last day at La Muse. By late afternoon, I'd come to the end of a good writing session. I stretched and heard voices coming from the kitchen.

'Right,' I said to myself. 'You've earned your supper tonight.' I tidied up my desk and went downstairs. Gillian and Ellie were piling the kitchen table with an incredible array of food.

'It's time for the big soup,' said Gillian. 'Three people went home this morning. Look at all the food they left us.'

'Wow,' I said. 'This will be amazing.'

We sorted the vegetables from the meat and the grains.

'There's only one way to get going,' said Gillian as she started chopping onions and garlic.

'I'll take care of these,' I said as I cut spicy sausages into small circular bites for frying.

'This can be the base,' said Lynn, who took a crockery bowl of white bean stew and poured it into a large stockpot.

'Can't forget wine,' said Adrian, who opened a red and a white and plunked them into the middle of the table with glasses.

We chopped and fried and sautéed and simmered our way to a big steaming pot of bean and vegetable soup with spicy chorizo and fresh herbs. The soup had something from everyone – present and past.

It was still warm enough to sit outside, so we carried the soup, bowls, bread, salad and wine to the stone patio. The sun was beginning its descent across the valley.

'Thanks to our departed friends,' said Gillian. 'Gone but not forgotten.'

'And to us, right here and now,' I added.

'We're all in the soup together,' said Ellie, wise beyond her years.

I felt a genuine connection – to the people at the table, to those who had left that morning, and beyond – to the family and friends and acquaintances and strangers I'd encountered with a new kind of openness in the past few years. During this time I had learned what it meant to live in the vividness of here, the peacefulness of now and in the kindness of our collective heart.

As the sun set behind the mountain across from a table on a stone patio in the south of France, there was a deep sense of community and a feeling of real affection. We'd shared a special place and time and experienced something akin to love. Now, it was time to say goodbye.

Postscript

May 2017

'You look great,' said my friend Lydia as she straightened the neckline of my gown. 'And so happy.'

'Thanks,' I said, giving her hand a squeeze. 'You too. Now, smile for the camera!'

We turned toward the photographer as he snapped the last few shots.

'Okay, all done!' he said with a thumbs-up. 'Now, you'd better get to the church. The ceremony starts in twenty minutes. I'll be waiting for you on the front steps.'

I reached down to pick up my things, and my gown fell off to the side again. It was a bit too big and pretty itchy. Still, I didn't mind. I caught up with the others as they turned onto University Avenue heading toward All Saints Cathedral. My stomach burbled to remind me that I hadn't eaten enough, and a tiny trickle of sweat ran down the back of my neck. 'Nerves,' I said to myself. 'Excited . . . and, happy.'

After arriving at the church and posing for a few more photographs, we assembled just inside the huge wooden doors. As the first notes of the processional hymn reverberated in the cavernous space, I inhaled the musky smell of centuries-old wood mingled with candles and incense. Sunlight slanted through stained glass, throwing beams of colour across the heads of the assembled guests. I took a deep breath, paused and made my first step down the aisle. The next few minutes – how many I'm not sure – passed in a blur. Then, I heard my name.

'Mary Jane Grant.'

I stepped forward and met the outstretched hand of the dean.

'Congratulations,' he said, shaking my hand as he presented my diploma.

'Thank you very much.' I accepted the large, white envelope and turned back toward my friends. After we'd all received our diplomas, the dean leaned into the microphone.

'Ladies and gentlemen. It is with great pleasure that I present to you the 2017 graduating class for the degree of Master of Fine Arts in Creative Writing.'

We cheered and clapped together – for ourselves and for one another, colleagues who had become friends over the last two years as we worked and wrote and read our words out loud for one another. 'Is it good enough?' we'd ask. 'Can you see the soft, hopeful shade of green that painted the side of the mountain I gazed at from my window in France? Can you hear the logs crackling in the fireplace that warmed the house that was my home for so many years? Do your taste buds tingle when I tell you about a tart burst of wild blueberry on my tongue?'

And what about the other words, those that sought to convey the gnawing pain of loss, or the lingering veil of sadness, or the faint flicker of love gone for good? We worked so hard to get those right, to capture the essence of our experiences and the elusiveness of our emotions. We'd do our best and then we'd meet in clusters of mismatched chairs in seminar rooms to read our work and seek one another's advice. We'd hope and wonder, 'Did it work? Did my heart cross this bridge of words to reach yours? Could you feel what I felt?'

I began my story in November 2013, when I found myself in an airport lounge, sat between a bored middle-aged couple and a seemingly carefree but careless girl. 'At least they knew where they fitted', I thought at the time. Untethered and adrift, I was no longer attached to the people, places and pastimes that had shaped my life. The dotted line that I had assumed would guide me toward a likely future had been erased. It was then that I decided I would write my way out of the past and into the next chapter of my life. To heal the old and create the new.

And so I, along with my new friends whose black gowns flapped in the cool breeze on that sunny day in May, elected to become writers and artists. Our stories were unique, but we shared the desire to turn life into art. Now, with diplomas in hand, we were ready to continue the challenge.

As we made our way down the aisle of the cathedral, I looked at the worn marble under my feet and thought about those who had walked here through the centuries, some overwhelmed with sorrow, others full of hope.

'Warm', I said to myself as a couple of tears rolled down my cheek.

'Happy,' I said as we walked out into the afternoon sun together.

Sources

Grateful acknowledgement is made to the following for permission to reprint excerpts from previously published material:

Ackerman, Diane, *A Natural History of the Senses* (Random House, New York, 1990)

Ban Breathnach, Sarah, *Simple Abundance* (Grand Central Publishing, New York, 1995)

Barnes, Julian, *Levels of Life* (Jonathan Cape, The Random House Group Limited, London, 2013)

Berry, Wendell, an excerpt from 'Healing' in *What Are People For?* (Counterpoint, Berkeley, 1990, 2010)

De Botton, Alain, *The Pleasures and Sorrows of Work* (Hamish Hamilton, Penguin Books, London, 2009)

Feynman, Richard, *The Pleasure of Finding Things Out* (Helix Books, Perseus Book Group, New York 1999)

Gilpin, Richard, *Mindfulness for Black Dogs and Blue Days* (Leaping Hare Press, Lewes, UK, 2012)

Graham, Martha, as quoted in *Martha: The Life and Work of Martha Graham* by Agnes de Mille (Random House, New York, 1991)

Gros, Frédéric, *A Philosophy of Walking* (Verso Books, London, 2014)

Hassed, Craig and Chambers, Richard, *Mindful Learning* (Shambhala Publications, Boston, 2014)

Hepola, Sarah, *Blackout: Remembering the Things I Drank to Forget* (Grand Central Publishing, Hachette Book Group, New York, 2015)

Kearney, Richard, *Carnal Hermeneutics* (Fordham University Press, New York, 2015)

Kearney, Richard, 'Losing our Touch' in *New York Times*, August 30, 2014

Killingsworth, Matthew and Gilbert, Daniel, 'A Wandering Mind is an Unhappy Mind', in *Science Magazine*, November 12, 2010, Vol. 330, Issue 6006, page 932

Lindbergh, Anne Morrow, *Gift from the Sea* (Chatto & Windus, London, 2015)

Nin, Anaïs, *The Diary of Anaïs Nin, Volume 3: 1939-1944* © 1966 by Anaïs Nin and renewed 1994 by Rupert Pole. Used by permission of Houghton Mifflin Harcourt Publishing Company. All rights reserved.

Norris, Daniel, quoted on the website Lifeedited.com, February 11, 2015

Parkin, John, *F**k It: The Ultimate Spiritual Way* (Hay House, London, 2007, 2008, 2014)

Reichl, Ruth, *My Kitchen Year: 136 Recipes That Saved My Life* (Appetite by Random House, Canada 2015)

Rilke, Rainer Maria, as quoted in *Rilke's Book of Hours: Love Poems to God* edited by Anita Barrows and Joanna Macy (Riverhead Books, a division of Penguin Putnam, New York, 1996)

Sacks, Oliver, *Gratitude* (Alfred A. Knopf, New York, 2015)

Shihab Nye, Naomi, an excerpt from 'Kindness' in *Words Under the Words: Selected Poems* (Far Corner Books, 1994)

Solnit, Rebecca, *Wanderlust* (Granta Books, London, 2014)

Susanka, Sarah, *The Not So Big Life* (Random House, New York, 2007)

Thoreau, Henry David, *The Journal, 1837–1861*, Volume XXIX, April 24, 1859, edited by Damion Searls (New York Review Books, New York, 2009)

Watts, Alan, *The Wisdom of Insecurity: A Message for an Age of Anxiety*, 1951 (Second Vintage Books Edition, Random House, 2011)

Whitman, Walt, 'Carol of Occupations' in *Leaves of Grass*, 1900 (public domain)

Whyte, David, *Consolations: The Solace, Nourishment and Underlying Meaning of Everyday Words* (Many Rivers Press, Langley WA, 2015)

Wolfe, Thomas, *Thomas Wolfe's Letters to his Mother* (Charles Scribner's Sons, New York, 1943)

Acknowledgements

Sincere thanks to my agent Jane Graham-Maw and my editor Hannah Black, whose vision and expertise helped bring this book to life.

I would also like to acknowledge the faculty and staff from the MFA program in Creative Nonfiction at the University of King's College in Halifax, Canada. For their skillful advice and encouragement, I'd like to thank my mentors – Lorri Neilsen Glenn, Ken McGoogan, Lori A. May, and earlier at the University of Toronto, Beth Kaplan. I'm grateful to be part of a small group of talented and generous MFA alumni who continue to meet to share mutual support and insightful feedback.

In my life I have been blessed with an extraordinary extended family and a wide-ranging group of wonderful friends. We've been through it all together, and I look forward to our ongoing journey.

My childhood story belongs not only to me but to my brother and my sisters. For their generosity of spirit and lifelong support, I am truly grateful.

I am especially lucky to have travelled through life in the company of the most amazing female friends. The laughs still outnumber the tears – and together we are ready for anything, anytime.

Special thanks to my son for being a constant source of inspiration and for challenging me to look at life in new and different ways.

And to my husband for believing in me, pure and simple.

End Notes

This story is based on events from my life. In a few instances, I have combined events or compressed timelines. Personal names and descriptions have been changed and, in some cases, composite characters have been created to protect people's privacy.